SOME
NINETEENTH CENTURY
COMPOSERS

Some Nineteenth Century Composers

by
John Horton

Geoffrey Cumberlege
OXFORD UNIVERSITY PRESS
LONDON   NEW YORK   TORONTO
1950

Oxford University Press, Amen House, London E.C.4

GLASGOW   NEW YORK   TORONTO   MELBOURNE   WELLINGTON

BOMBAY   CALCUTTA   MADRAS   CAPE TOWN

Geoffrey Cumberlege, Publisher to the University

PRINTED IN GREAT BRITAIN BY
ROBERT CUNNINGHAM AND SONS LTD., ALVA

CONTENTS

	PAGE
INTRODUCTION	vii
MENDELSSOHN	I
LISZT	12
SMETANA	24
BORODIN	32
RIMSKY-KORSAKOV	39
GRIEG	47
FRANCK	55
SAINT-SAËNS	62
FAURÉ	70
DEBUSSY	79
ELGAR	88
MAHLER	96

INTRODUCTION

THIS book was written in response to a request to deal with twelve nineteenth-century composers who had not been included already in Mr. Eric Blom's *Some Great Composers*, nor were to be included in a future volume (now in preparation), devoted to opera composers. For this reason the contents list may appear somewhat capriciously drawn up. Yet the very process of selecting the team, as well as the subsequent writing, has compelled me to fit the various chapters mentally into a framework, about which the reader may care to know.

First, every composer treated here bears in some degree the stamp of nationalism, one of the strongest characteristics of nineteenth century music. Even the two members of the Jewish race (but professing the Christian faith) who begin and end the list were coloured by the traditions and culture of the lands in which they were born. Mendelssohn is primarily a North German composer, Mahler essentially an Austrian one. It is curious that those who gave loudest voice to their nationalist sympathies—Liszt, with his pride in his Hungarian origins, and Saint-Saëns as a prominent leader of the French revival—were the most cosmopolitan in their range of personal style. On the other hand, even those who were most completely under the spell of national idioms used as the foundations of their musical grammar and syntax the language of Beethoven and Berlioz. This is markedly true of the most original and successful of the Slavonic composers in our list: Smetana and Borodin, whose greatness lies not so much in a cult of regionalism as in their power of expressing themselves in new and virile dialects of the universal musical language of the period. We have at last begun to get rid of the kind of prejudice that regards Borodin's B minor Symphony as provincial in relation to Schubert's, or *The Bartered Bride* in relation to *Der Freischütz*. The truth now appears to us only too clearly that Europe between 1814 and 1914 was culturally one in a way that it had never been before and unhappily has never been since, and that a work of genius created in any region of it could, within a generation at most, become part of the heritage of the rest.

It is also illuminating to try ranging some of these composers around one of them, Franz Liszt, and to study the impact of his personality on theirs. Most of them met Liszt at one time or another, heard him talk and heard him play, were made to play to him, were advised and encouraged by him. Grieg, Saint-Saëns, Borodin, and Smetana were indebted to him for friendship and professional aid given freely at critical stages of their careers. Each received an exhortation to the same effect—that the composer should follow the path his instinct had directed him to take, fear nothing from his more conservative critics, and assert his individuality. In spite of his championship of Wagner, Liszt was no idolator of German music, and he lent a willing ear to the young men who brought something new from Bohemia's woods and fields, the steppes of Central Asia, or the mountain and the fjord. With French music he was even more closely in sympathy. What, in the days of his youth, he took from Berlioz he gave back to France in the days of his maturity through Saint-Saëns. He could enter into the French delight in the dramatic, the festive, and the picturesque in music, and the hard, polished finish of his own style is typical of French workmanship. Of the younger French composers, Fauré and Debussy passed swiftly and transitorily across Liszt's orbit. Franck's wonderful extemporisation on his organ at Ste. Clothilde astonished the first keyboard executant of the age, who went away declaring that in Franck the spirit of J. S. Bach lived again. Technically, not only the music of Franck himself but also modern French music as a whole owes much to Liszt's later style, with its remarkable innovations in keyboard figuration, its breadth of harmonic vocabulary, and its experiments in theme-transformation and cyclic form. Its ininfluence on the Russian 'Mighty Handful', of which Borodin and Rimsky-Korsakov were members, is even more important, being exerted both directly through his contacts with Borodin and Balakirev (the mentor of Rimsky-Korsakov) but also indirectly through the mutual interest that existed between Liszt and Glinka, the father of Russian music.

In another sense Liszt is a key-man of the century. His great and complex personality was the battle-ground of a conflict that affected every notable composer of the period, from Mendelssohn to Mahler. In the eighteenth century, and for that matter during the whole previous history of the art, the functions of composer and executant were regarded as one, or at any rate as not difficult to combine in a single person. The nineteenth century, with its enormous expansion of public performance, developments in instrumental technique, insistence on exact and sensitive interpretation, combined with the romantic conception of the composer's preeminence as the bearer of a 'message', upset a balance which has never been restored. The path to the conductor's rostrum is strewn with the unfulfilled careers of promising composers. The economic aspect of the problem has also to be taken into account. The disappearance of private musical establishments meant that a musician could no longer earn a livelihood by composing. He must enter the highly competitive field of the executant, build up a formidable technique, and, assuming that he found favour with the public, spend most of his life travelling about the world repeating his early successes. As an alternative, or as a supplementary source of income, he could teach. In either case his creative work had to be relegated to vacations, or to other times of leisure or even indisposition. Mendelssohn was one of the earliest to feel this drain on his creative powers. 'When one is no longer young,' he told the English critic Chorley a few months before his death in 1847, 'one should not go about playing and concert-giving', and he expressed his strong wish '. . . of settling down somewhere in the Rhine Land, not in any town, there to devote himself more eagerly than ever to composition.' This reminds us of Mahler's confession of 'moments of discouragement in which I should like to give up music altogether and . . . pass a quiet, unregarded existence in some peaceful corner of the earth. It is above all this dreadful treadmill of the theatre that crushes my soul.'[1] It is interesting to note how the other composers in our list reacted to the dual claims of creation and interpretation. Smetana had the question settled for him by the misfortune of his deafness, Rimsky-Korsakov by his late start as a serious musician. Borodin found a unique solution in his capacity to excel in two different professions simultaneously. Grieg had to run a lifelong gauntlet of his own early works. Debussy also became a specialist performer of his own music, though not a very complaisant one. Elgar, with his unerring rightness in personal decisions, rejected the success he had been promised as a concert violinist. But it was Liszt, as always, who made the grand and spectacular gesture. At the age of thirty-seven, after winning such renown as no solo artist had ever before achieved—unless it were Paganini—Liszt renounced all its grosser temptations and distractions. It is true that he lingers in popular legend as the concert virtuoso *par excellence*; but to the musician of to-day, and especially to the composer of to-day, it is his creative genius that matters above everything.

Spring 1950

---

[1] Quoted in Mosco Carner: *Of Men and Music*, London, 1944.

MENDELSSOHN

'MUSIC has here buried a rich treasure, but still fairer hopes.' The epitaph on Schubert's grave might also have been placed over that of Felix Mendelssohn, though with different meaning. For Mendelssohn's misfortune was not so much in that, like Schubert, he failed to grow old in years, as that he failed to remain young in spirit. No musician, not even Mozart, began life with greater promise. Besides possessing an extraordinary musical talent he was endowed with many other gifts, physical, intellectual, and artistic. He was brought up in a home where wealth and culture were abundant and happily proportioned. His abilities were discovered early and fostered lovingly. He might, if his early training had been otherwise, have chosen to pass his life in the reflected glory of Moses Mendelssohn, his grandfather, and one of the greatest Jews of modern times. Moses, whose portrait can be recognised in Lessing's *Nathan der Weise*, did more than any man to raise the Jewish race in German-speaking countries to a level of esteem it was to occupy for a century and a half after the philosopher's death in 1786. Moses Mendelssohn's second son, Abraham, adopted the banking profession and married Lea Solomon, whose dark eyes, linguistic gifts, and above all musical talents were to be inherited by all her children. The family lived until 1811 in Hamburg, where the first three children of Abraham and Lea were born: Fanny, Felix (born 3rd February

1809), and Rebecca. When Hamburg was occupied by the French forces the Mendelssohns moved to Berlin and the parents devoted themselves in earnest to the education of the children (a fourth, Paul, was born in 1813), all of whom they had decided to bring up in the Christian religion. In this course they were supported by the example of other members of the family, one of whom, Lea's brother, had on baptism taken the surname Bartholdy and advised Abraham to do likewise. There is no reason to doubt the integrity of Abraham's motives for rejecting the faith of his ancestors; his father's humanistic philosophy had revealed much common ground between Judaism and Christianity, and the Lutheran articles of belief have not a few contacts with Jewish religion and ethics. For example, Felix Mendelssohn, like Saul of Tarsus, must be capable of earning his livelihood by his own toil, and must be prepared to give an exact account of his stewardship. He must reverence Holy Writ and base all his actions on serious motives. 'We must deny ourselves at every moment of our lives' wrote Felix in his confirmation essay; 'How could we learn anything in our youth, unless we did without things and turned our backs on tempting pleasures and kept to our work?'

Abraham made sure that there should be work in plenty. He engaged Zelter, director of the Berlin Singakademie, as his son's composition teacher; Ludwig Berger built up his impeccable piano technique; the scholar K. W. L. Heyse directed his general studies. This educational scheme, though rigorous, was broadly based and even included athletic exercises. Felix displayed effortless proficiency in every branch of his studies. He attended a course of lectures in the University of Berlin, and whetted his intellectual appetite with the conversation of the distinguished guests who frequented his father's house. In 1825 Abraham bought No. 3 Leipzigerstrasse, an ample residence whose garden-house was the meeting place, every Sunday morning, of some of the most illustrious figures in European art and letters: Weber and Heine, Spohr and Hegel, Paganini and Thorvaldsen were at various times among the company. At these Sunday meetings the Mendelssohns and their friends made music, and Felix had his earliest opportunities of becoming known as pianist and composer. Of the quantity of music he produced in his early teens the three Quartets for Piano and Strings (Ops. 1, 2, and 3) and the Sonata for Violin and Piano (Op. 4) were approved by Zelter as worthy of publication.

The Op. 3 Piano Quartet was dedicated to the seventy-three-year old Goethe, with whom Felix spent a fortnight during the autumn of 1821 at his home in Weimar. Of how Felix was entertained there, of the compliments Goethe paid him, and of the recitals of Bach, Mozart, and Beethoven, with improvisations of his own, that he gave in return, we can read in some of the earliest of the vivid, high-spirited letters that flowed as readily as musical scores from Mendelssohn's pen. The works of the next five years show him as a mature artist; indeed, he never surpassed and often fell below the level of the Octet for Strings (Op. 20) and the Overture to *A Midsummer Night's*

Dream. To apply Matthew Arnold's famous distinction, the 'Hellenising' influences on Mendelssohn's spirit were stronger than the 'Hebraising' at this period. He was allowed to see much of the world, and found it very good. In 1822 he had spent a holiday with his family in Switzerland and in the Spring of 1825 he accompanied his father to Paris, where he charmed even the aged and irascible Cherubini. Mendelssohn for his part was shocked by the French neglect of Beethoven's works and almost complete ignorance of J. S. Bach's; his own A minor String Quartet (Op. 13) is a token of his reverence for both of those masters. Zelter had fired him with love for Bach's clavier, organ, and choral music, and on the 11th March 1829 the youth of twenty was to make musical history by giving a performance of the St. Matthew Passion, the first since Bach himself directed it at Leipzig a hundred years before.

That same Spring, Felix was in London, like Haydn winning admirers in aristocratic households and friends in middle-class ones. Scotland also had to be visited, since 'Ossian' and Walter Scott had endeared it to the romantic imagination. Among the Hebrides Mendelssohn found the inspiration for a Concert Overture, several times renamed and finally given a local habitation as *Fingal's Cave*, and in the roofless chapel of Holyrood it pleased him to jot down the first bars of a *Scottish Symphony*. These works, together with the *Midsummer Night's Dream* Overture, give point to Wagner's comparison of Mendelssohn's instrumental style to water-colour painting; the lines are clear, the orchestral colours delicate, the lights and shadows gently contrasted.

Mendelssohn's wander-years were not yet over. He had still to visit two of the great homelands of European music, South Germany and Italy. He found the musical glory of Italy in sad decline. Orchestral playing scarcely existed, and even the Papal Choir proved disappointing. It was his eyes, rather than his ears, that were fascinated by the life and colour of Naples and Rome. 'Why', he wrote, 'should Italy still insist on being the land of art, while in reality it is the land of nature, and so delights every heart?' As not uncommonly happens with a sensitive, creative temperament, unfamiliar scenes gave fresh meanings to those already visited, and under the Italian sun Mendelssohn was busy with sound-impressions inspired by northern lands. He made arrangements of Lutheran chorales, developed his sketches for *The Hebrides* and the *Scottish Symphony*, and in *The First Walpurgis Night* produced a picturesque choral and orchestral setting of an episode from Goethe's *Faust*. In contrast to the rain-drenched visions of the Hebrides and the lurid mists of the Brocken gleam the Mediterranean white and azure of the *Italian Symphony*. And it was probably his tour in the south that set Mendelssohn searching for an opera-text; the quest was never completed, for his conditions were exacting: 'Deutsch müsste es sein, und adel und rein'—German, noble, and pure.

Mendelssohn prolonged his tour by visiting part of Switzerland and the Rhine and arrived towards the end

B

of 1831 in Paris, then at the height of its artistic glory. Paganini was there, and Chopin, and Liszt. Cherubini still reigned grimly over the Conservatoire and the Opera, though Rossini, Auber, and Meyerbeer were in the ascendant. Habeneck was atoning for the Parisians' earlier neglect of the great German classics, and under his leadership Mendelssohn played Beethoven's G major Concerto. The Paris salons welcomed Mendelssohn's own instrumental works: some of the early String Quartets and Piano Quartets, the *Midsummer Night's Dream* Overture, and the *Reformation* Symphony in which his treatment of the Lutheran Hymn 'Ein fest' Burg' found an echo a few years later when Meyerbeer wrote *Les Huguenots*. These Paris successes were followed by a second visit to England.

Mendelssohn's return to Berlin in June 1832 may be taken as marking the end not only of his creative springtime but also of his artistic freedom. Abraham Mendelssohn's dignified ambition, as well as his own ingrained sense of responsibility, demanded that he should find a salaried post. He was disappointed in an attempt to obtain the conductorship of the Singakademie in succession to Zelter, who had lately died, but in May 1833 he received an invitation to conduct the Lower Rhine Festival at Düsseldorf, and subsequently to become Director of Music to that town for a term of three years. This appointment gave him scope for the strong interest in choral singing he had gained under Zelter and strengthened by his researches into the works of Bach and Handel. He was already at work on his first oratorio, *St. Paul*, doubt-

less stimulated by his contacts with English oratorio singing and by some conversations he had been having with
Marx, Director of Music in Berlin University, on the
choice of oratorio texts. Fortunately the terms of his contract with the Düsseldorf authorities allowed him time
for composition. All the same, the post was an onerous
one. As the centre of the most thickly populated part of
Germany, Düsseldorf could show a wide variety of musical enterprises. Besides the choral singing already mentioned there was an opera house, there were orchestral
concerts, and there were Catholic churches with choral
services on an imposing scale. No musician of Mendelssohn's calibre could have failed to revel in these opportunities, and there is no doubt that the Düsseldorf period
was beneficial not only to Mendelssohn's personality but
also to the quality of North German music for many years
to come. Mendelssohn was one of the first of the line of
modern virtuoso conductors, building an international reputation on a solid foundation of talent, scholarship, and
the power to impose his own high standards on others.
There is little doubt, however, that Mendelssohn's inter-
pretative abilities were exercised at the expense of his creative talent, which declines from this time onwards. The
successes he achieved in conducting at Düsseldorf brought
invitations to direct concerts and festivals at Aachen, at
Cologne, and finally at the Leipzig Gewandhaus.

In control of the famous concerts whose lineage dated
to the year 1743 and whose first conductor had been J. F.
Doles, a pupil of J. S. Bach, Mendelssohn secured a qual-

ity of orchestral playing that surprised not only the rank and file of the Leipzig audiences but also an experienced critic like Robert Schumann, who had at first been a little disturbed by Mendelssohn's practice of using the baton in the modern way instead of leading the orchestra from the principal violin desk. As usual, Mendelssohn's popularity was almost universal. But in the midst of his new work, and his new friendships with the Schumanns, Chopin, Liszt, Moscheles and others, he suffered the first real sorrow of his life. Abraham Mendelssohn, to whom his son had always looked as 'his instructor in art and in life', died, and Felix was oppressed with a sense of solitude in the midst of throngs of admirers. 'The only thing that now remains,' he wrote, 'is to do one's duty.' He toiled to finish the oratorio, *St. Paul*, on which Abraham had placed such hopes, and which was destined for the Lower Rhine Festival of 1836. He bade farewell to his carefree youth with a new version of the Overture, *Melusine*.

In the Spring of 1837 he married Cécile Jeanrenaud, daughter of a Lutheran pastor of Frankfurt. She shared his love of romantic scenery, of sketching, and of genial domesticity. His reviving spirits found expression in the E minor and E flat major String Quartets (Op. 44, Nos. 2 and 3), an Autumn visit to England to conduct the Birmingham Festival brought him fresh honours, and he felt able once more to throw himself into the multifarious activities of his Leipzig appointment. This, though entailing drudgery like rehearsing interminable symphonies by undistinguished Kapellmeisters, also carried with it memorable experiences such as the first performance of Schubert's great C major Symphony, recently brought to light by Schumann from among a pile of manuscripts in Vienna. Mendelssohn's enthusiasm for Bach increased as he worked under the shadow of the Thomaskirche; he organised a movement to erect a statue in memory of the great Cantor, and set himself to master the greater organ works of Bach and, to some extent, to found his own compositions for the organ upon Bach's. He identified himself with one of the leading commercial activities of the town by writing the *Hymn of Praise* (Lobgesang) in celebration of the supposed four-hundredth anniversary of the invention of printing, and for this received the public thanks of the King of Saxony. An invitation from the King of Prussia to administer the musical side of a new Academy of Arts in Berlin was reluctantly accepted, and together with a brief and informal visit to England, where he was charmingly received by Queen Victoria and the Prince Consort, broke the round of duties in Leipzig. On the 3rd April 1843 he was the principal figure at the opening of the Leipzig Conservatorium, an institution that was to be the nursery of some of the best talent of Europe and America during the next half century. Mendelssohn's heart was neither in teaching nor in administration, but by dint of insisting on artistic integrity as the first principle of a school of music he established a tradition that even pedantry in the years to come could not entirely destroy.

If Mendelssohn had remained, like Bach, undisturbed

at Leipzig, he might have found ways of reconciling his official duties with his composing. His pen was still active; in fulfilment of a commission from the King of Prussia he had returned to *A Midsummer Night's Dream* and supplemented the Overture with a number of delicate and humorous pieces of incidental music. The Cello Sonata in D (Op. 58) was also written at this time, the Violin Concerto was in preparation for Ferdinand David, the leader of the Gewandhaus orchestra, and the oratorio *Elijah* was well advanced. What wore out his delicate nervous system was the constant demands that kept coming from Berlin, where he was still nominally Director of Music to the King of Prussia, and from populous and music-loving regions like the Rhineland and England. *Elijah* was performed for the first time at the Birmingham Festival on the 26th August 1846. He left England as a tired man, satiated with applause and flattery and longing for peace and leisure. He had already delegated his responsibility as Director of the Leipzig Conservatorium to Moscheles and his duties as conductor of the Gewandhaus concerts to the young Danish musician, Gade. But his wish was not to be granted. Returning in September 1847 from his tenth visit to England, he heard that his favourite sister Fanny, a woman scarcely less gifted than himself and the partner of his early studies, had died suddenly during one of the Sunday rehearsals at the Leipzigerstrasse. The shock was mortal in its effect on him. Some have found in the F minor String Quartet (Op. 80), written soon afterwards, the note of personal grief. His own illness grew upon him; like a premonition he seemed to hear the command 'Halt! No further!' On the 3rd November 1847 he had a cerebral hemorrhage like those that had carried off his father and his sister, and on the following day he died in his thirty-ninth year.

LISZT

Few people are now left alive to tell of the picturesque and romantic appearance of the 'Abbé' Liszt or recall his unique prowess at the keyboard. He died before the sound-recording machine had grown out of its experimental stage. A handful of his compositions belongs to that musical limbo which one calls—according to one's upbringing—either 'popular' or 'classical': the *Liebesträume* and the *Consolations*, a few of the Hungarian Rhapsodies, the Hungarian Fantasia, and the first Piano Concerto. On these are based the concept of Liszt as a purveyor of suave, Byronic melodies, succulent harmonies, and pyrotechnic keyboard passage-writing. It is to other aspects of his work, however, that the serious musician now turns, to find in them much that is prophetic of the music of the twentieth century: to the Symphonic Poems, prototypes of many a modern orchestral piece, to the poetical *Années de pèlerinage*, forerunners of impressionism, to the tremendous, fervid Piano Sonata and the Symphonies that evoke the spirits of Dante and Goethe.

Destiny seems to have resolved to make a musician of Franz (or Ferencz) Liszt, even to the point of causing him to be born, on the 22nd October 1811, on the Esterházy estate where Josef Haydn had lived and worked up to twenty years earlier. In later life Liszt made much capital out of his Hungarian origins and prided himself on keeping in touch with both the nobility and the peasantry of

Hungary; but modern research workers, including Bartók and Kodály, have shown that he had but a superficial, and often incorrect, knowledge of Hungarian folk-song, and that most of the tunes in the so-called Hungarian Rhapsodies are of Gipsy rather than Hungarian provenance.

Liszt's musical education was orthodox enough. After some instruction from his father, who besides being a steward on the Esterházy estate was a competent amateur pianist, and after some local success as a prodigy, he was sent to Vienna. There he became a pupil of the aged Salieri, and of the famous pianist Czerny, who was so much impressed by the boy's talent that he undertook to teach him without fee. Soon Franz was astonishing the critical audiences of Vienna, attracting the attention of Beethoven, and, at the age of eleven, contributing, along with Schubert, Czerny, Hummel, Moscheles and other noted musicians of the day, to a set of variations on a waltz by Diabelli.

In 1823 Liszt's father carried him off on a concert tour of German cities, and finally to Paris where, failing to enter the boy as a student at the Conservatoire—foreigners were ineligible—he secured as teacher the veteran Anton Reicha, who had been a pupil of Michael Haydn and a colleague of Beethoven (in the Elector's orchestra at Bonn), and was to live on to give César Franck some of his earliest composition lessons. Franz Liszt came to him as something more than a brilliant pupil; he was already an international virtuoso and could already challenge the greatest pianists of the time (Hummel alone, it was said, surpassed him). His conquest of Paris was soon complete, and was followed by three visits to London. He played at the Argyll Rooms and Drury Lane Theatre, laying the foundations of a reputation in this country that was to endure, in spite of some Puritanical head-shaking over his later moral courses, for the next sixty years.

Soon after visiting London for the third time (in 1827) Liszt lost his father, and turned for a means of livelihood to the salons of Paris, where his natural courtliness, as much as his technical distinction, made him socially acceptable and ensured him plenty of professional engagements and pupils. Already he had begun to show the contradictions of his nature: at one moment the *bon viveur*, at another the religious ascetic, withdrawing from gay society to seek solitude and contemplation. But for a time the worldly aspect predominated. To an artist, the French capital was never more stimulating than in the third decade of the nineteenth century. It was the home of Ingres and Delacroix, Balzac and Heine, Chopin, Berlioz, Bellini, Rossini, Meyerbeer, and Paganini, the last of whom Liszt admired above all for his unending quest for technical mastery and perhaps also for the aura of diabolical mystery that surrounded him. As yet Liszt was little regarded as a composer; but he excelled in transcribing and performing other men's music, arranging for piano such intractable works as Berlioz' *Symphonie fantastique*, and giving magnificent readings of Beethoven, Schubert, Weber, and those who interested him among his contemporaries, particularly Schumann, Chopin, and Mendelssohn.

In 1833 began one of the most serious and lasting of Liszt's many affairs of the heart. He met the Comtesse d'Agoult, a woman six years older than himself and married to a middle-aged husband. In 1835 they took refuge together in Geneva, and there their first daughter Blandine was born. For the first time in his life, since his brilliant public career began, Liszt had time and leisure for composition in the true sense, as distinct from the writing down of improvisations and arrangements. His impressions of Swiss scenery and legend, entitled *Album d'un voyageur* and dating from 1835, are better known in their revised form in the first part of the *Années de pèlerinage*. The Italian section of the *Années* originated in another tour Liszt made with the Comtesse, this time in Italy, where their second daughter Cosima—destined to become the wife first of von Bülow, and afterwards of Wagner—was born. Once again the absence from the distractions of Paris resulted in solid achievement: this time the twelve *Études d'exécution transcendente* were completed and revised, and the Six Studies based on Paganini's Caprices for the violin were written, the two collections forming a kind of compendium of Liszt's keyboard technique as developed up to this time. He also produced a work of deeper significance, the *Fantasia quasi sonata*, *Après une lecture du Dante*, which was ultimately included in the *Années de pèlerinage*. His stay in Italy was interrupted by news of the disastrous Danube floodings in Hungary. Touched by the plight of the inhabitants, he hurried to Vienna and gave a series of recitals in aid of

the relief fund. Resuming his Italian tour with the Comtesse he went on to Rome, where he struck up a friendship
with Ingres, then Director of the Villa Medici, who pain-
ted Liszt's portrait.

By the end of 1839 Liszt was again in Vienna. He had
parted for the time being from the Comtesse and her growing family—a third child had been born in Italy—and he
had entered a new phase of his career. It was now that
his renown as a wizard of the keyboard was built up in
earnest. As for his compositions, they were still represented mainly in his recitals by dazzling technical studies
and masterly transcriptions of operatic and orchestral
works. Nowadays such things hardly seem to have been
worth the playing or the hearing; then they were irresistible, for they brought into the salon or concert hall much
that was novel and unique. The originals of the transcriptions, for one thing, were less easily accessible than
they are in these days of broadcasting, the gramophone,
miniature scores, and widespread public concerts. Frequently the only way of getting to know a large-scale
orchestral work was through the medium of a two- or
four-hand piano transcription, and even a popular favourite
like the Overture to *William Tell* was much played in this
way by amateurs. Secondly, Liszt's transcriptions were
sui generis—no mere hack-work, but satisfying piano pieces
in their own right. Thirdly, the idea of one man giving an
evening's entertainment and producing these magnificent
torrents of sound was not over-familiar: even the piano-
forte itself was still in process of evolution, and Liszt had

worked out, not only by dint of genius but also through hours of study and experiment, a technical equipment that enabled him to exceed in range of brilliance, power, colour, and sweetness anything that the older virtuosi— Czerny, Cramer, Hummel, Moscheles, Thalberg, even Chopin—had been able to offer. Finally, there was the personality of the performer himself, swaying any gathering of people, small or great, that he chose to enter, and destined to establish the type of the 'inspired musician' of popular fancy for several generations to come.

From Vienna, Liszt made a characteristic return to the country of his birth, being received in Budapest with every mark of honour the lively Hungarian imagination could devise. Thence he travelled by way of Prague and Leipzig (where he had meetings with Mendelssohn and Schumann) to London, and played at Buckingham Palace. Much of the fortune he amassed by his recitals in England, and later in France and Germany, he had earmarked for the Beethoven memorial fund. He spent lavishly on his own expensive tastes and habits ('I have sixty waistcoats', he boasted) and made liberal allowances to the Comtesse d'Agoult, with whom he passed several vacations on the romantic island of Nonnewerth, in the Rhine.

By the Spring of 1842 Liszt was in Petersburg, a visit momentous for the future of Russian music; among those who attended his recitals were Stassov, Serov, and Glinka, all three of whom were to become corner-stones of the Russian nationalist school. Russia was not the only country on the fringes of Europe that heard Liszt during these restless, victorious years of his middle life. Towards the end of 1845 he was in Spain and Portugal, in 1846 he played to the Sultan in Constantinople. His travels culminated in another tour of Russia which brought about, in the ancient city of Kiev, his fateful meeting with the Princess Carolyne of Sayn-Wittgenstein, a wealthy young aristocrat who lived alone on her vast estates, surrounded by an army of serfs. In Liszt's dominating talent and personality she found a match for her own high degree of intelligence, and Liszt in his turn was attracted not only by the breadth of knowledge but also by the artistic sympathies he discovered in her. He had long since tired of the Comtesse d'Agoult, and readily fell in with the Princess's proposal that she should obtain a divorce from her husband and follow Liszt to Weimar, where he was about to take up a residential appointment as Musical Director to the Grand Duke of Saxe-Weimar.

This decision opened another fresh chapter in Liszt's life. At the age of thirty-six, and at the peak of his reputation as a virtuoso, he retired from professional activity, playing thereafter only as a concession to the public and never for a fee. The post he had accepted at Weimar carried with it a modest salary; on the other hand, his contract allowed him to live elsewhere for three-quarters of the year.

His duties during the season he was obliged to spend in Weimar were congenial enough. He enjoyed the novel experience of applying his talents to the production of

opera, reviving little known works, such as the operas of
Gluck, and drawing upon the whole of the grand and
comic repertory of the period. He smoothed the path of
new and difficult works and above all supported Wagner,
whose *Lohengrin* received its first performance at Weimar
in 1850. Liszt would have gone on to produce also *Tristan*
and *The Ring* had not the Duke drawn the purse-strings
tight and refused to sponsor such costly ventures. Liszt's
missionary zeal was not restricted to opera. He introduced
or reintroduced a large number of choral and orchestral
works of importance, including Beethoven's Ninth Symphony, Handel's *Messiah*, Schumann's *Paradise and the
Peri*, and Berlioz' *Damnation of Faust*. His growing interest in the orchestra led him to compose a series of twelve
Symphonic Poems, some of them, like *Mazeppa*, adapta-
tions of earlier piano pieces, others entirely new. All are
founded on some pictorial or poetical idea: *Les Préludes*
and the *Mountain Symphony* (*Ce qu'on entend sur la mon-
tagne*) were inspired by poems of Lamartine and Hugo,
The Ideal by a poem of Schiller, and *The Battle of the Huns*
by a popular picture by Kaulbach. In these works Liszt
is the father of a new species of instrumental composition,
familiar enough to us to-day through the symphonic poems
of Tchaikovsky, Richard Strauss, Saint-Saëns, Elgar and
others. The *Faust* and *Dante* Symphonies, both written
in the 1850's and both with choral endings, are also revolu-
tionary in their way and foreshadow the symphonic experiments of Mahler.

The strange ménage of the Villa Altenburg in Weimar,

where Liszt and the Princess occupied their own suites of rooms and for twelve years entertained a constant succession of famous people, must have made a remarkable contrast to the dignified, orderly life of the little town, with its hallowed memories of Goethe and Schiller. Equally incongruous is the showiness of the fifteen *Hungarian Rhapsodies* revised and published during the Weimar period. Liszt paid further tribute to the land of his birth in the readable, though unscholarly, monograph on *The gypsies and their music in Hungary*. The still unbroken, if somewhat diminished, popularity of the *Rhapsodies* is shared by some smaller pieces written in the 1850's: the *Harmonies poétiques et religieuses*, the *Liebesträume*,[1] and the *Valse impromptu*. On an entirely different plane, and related to the *Faust* and *Dante* Symphonies, is the great Piano Sonata in B minor.

In 1858 Liszt resigned from his post at Weimar. His ostensible reason for this step was the Duke's refusal, already mentioned, to sponsor the production of Wagner's later music-dramas. Liszt's private circumstances, however, probably had not a little to do with his change of plans. The Princess Wittgenstein now had firmer hopes of obtaining her divorce, and Liszt, with characteristic sense of theatrical effect, was hoping to marry her on his fiftieth birthday (22nd October 1861). The divorce entailed elaborate negotiations with the Vatican, and when the Princess went to Rome in 1860 to appeal in person Liszt followed her, only to learn on the eve of their wed-

[1] Piano transcriptions by Liszt of some of his own songs.

ding that the ecclesiastical authorities had after all refused
to sanction the divorce.

In the midst of his discomfiture and despondency Liszt
found his old longing for a life of religious contemplation
coming upon him anew. On the 25th April 1865 after
a period of preparation in a monastery, he was received
into the lower degrees of the Roman priesthood, and was
thenceforward known—somewhat inaccurately—as the
Abbé Liszt. The Princess also, in her own way, retired
from the follies of the world; she remained in Rome and
met Liszt from time to time, but most of her energies she
gave to the writing of an immensely long book on *The
Inner Causes of the Outward Weakness of the Church*. At
first Liszt lived within the Vatican; later he was given
quarters in the Villa d'Este at Tivoli, and divided his wak-
ing hours between the readings and meditations prescribed
for his new calling, and improvising and composing as vigorously as ever. Among the orchestral works dating from
this time are the two *Faust* Episodes—*The Night Ride*
and *Scene in a Village Inn*, often called the First Mephisto
Waltz. In contrast to these macabre fancies are ambitious
attempts to infuse new life into oratorio. *The Legend of
St. Elizabeth* and *Christus* are written on a large and flam-
boyant scale—the latter indeed is a trilogy rather than a
single work—and they exhibit the old blend of mysticism
and theatricality. In spite of his clerical robe and religious
exercises Liszt was still, in all sincerity, making the best
of both worlds.

Neither the cloister nor the study could hold him long.

C

In the summer of 1865 he was touring Hungary, in company with von Bülow, whom he counted one of his best pupils. In 1866 he was in Paris again. In 1867 he produced a Mass in Budapest for the coronation of Franz Josef. In 1869 he was persuaded to return to Weimar for three months of the year. A small house, the Hofgärtnerei, was assigned to him and soon became one of the chief focal points of European music. The months when he was not in residence at Weimar he would spend either in the Villa d'Este, whose pines and fountains are commemorated in two of his finest impressionist pieces, or, from 1875 onwards, in Budapest, where he presided over a newly-founded National Academy of Music. This Hungarian aspect of his life has received comparatively little attention, and the same is true of most of the compositions of his last years. They range from the set of miniatures called *The Christmas Tree* to the weird *Le lugubre gondole*, written shortly before the death of Wagner; and from the *Hungarian Portraits* to the last group of *Hungarian Rhapsodies* and the later choral music.

The last ten years of Liszt's life are filled with wanderings if anything more restless and extensive than those of his youth. His technical powers seemed to be unaffected by advancing age. At the approach of his seventy-fifth birthday he planned concert tours in Germany, Austria, France, Belgium, and England. This was his first visit to England for forty-five years. He met most of the celebrities of the time including Queen Victoria, Burne-Jones, Cardinal Manning, and Henry Irving. He also attended recitals by his pupils Walter Bache and Frederic Lamond. On his homeward journey he spent Holy Week among the churches of Antwerp, foregathered with Gounod and Saint-Saëns in Paris, and arrived in Bayreuth in time for the Wagner Festival. But he had taken a chill while travelling and although he dragged himself to a performance of *Tristan* he could not maintain the fight against pneumonia. On the 31st July 1886 he died. It is said that the last word on his lips was 'Tristan'; if so, it was characteristic of his extraordinary nature to recall at the last the achievements of another man. Never have sublime egotism and magnificent generosity been more strangely interwoven.

SMETANA

PEOPLE to whom Czechoslovakia is a 'far-off country' are sometimes surprised to learn that Smetana rather than Dvořák is regarded by the Czechs as their supreme national composer. But much of the Bohemian flavour we find so attractive in Dvořák's music was taken over from his older countryman; in the use of native dance-rhythms, especially, and of a type of melody that follows the cadences of folk-tune Smetana left little for his successors to do but to imitate him. On the other hand, whereas Dvořák produced a considerable body of orchestral and chamber music which can be heard with pleasure by those who know not a word of Czech beyond *dumka* and *furiant*, Smetana's finest work was put into the series of operas he wrote to Czech libretti for the national stage. Of these operas, only *The Bartered Bride* has so far been successfully transplanted to other lands. To appreciate Smetana to the full one must no doubt be steeped in Czech literature, legend, and history and possess an idiomatic knowledge of the language. Yet the foundations of his art rest upon the traditions of European music that we all share, and as his works become more accessible their broad humanity will impress itself on us in spite of the language barrier.

Bedřich Smetana was born at Litomysl in the southeast of Bohemia on the 2nd March 1824. He was the son of a brewer, who managed a business owned by Count Waldstein. The boy took to the violin and the piano with

an alacrity and success not uncommon in a land where
music was and still is part of the everyday life of the village and small town. At six he is said to have played in
public a piano arrangement of the overture to Auber's
La Muette de Portici, and in his early teens he was known
throughout the district for his brilliant performances of
pieces by Liszt, Thalberg, Henselt and other favourite
virtuosi of the day. Meanwhile, his general education followed the usual lines of middle and upper class education
in Bohemia at that time. It was carried on entirely in
German, and even in middle age Smetana was unable to
write his native language fluently. In Prague, where he
went to complete his school course, he took advanced lessons in piano-playing and formed a string quartet which
performed some of his earliest attempts at composition.
A polka, *Aus dem studentischen Leben* (1842), belongs to
this period and shows his early-awakened interest in the
national dance-form. It may have been the musical distractions of the capital that caused his father to remove
him to a high school at Pilsen (Plzeň). But his mind was
made up to a musical career, and after a term of service
as music-master in the household of Count Leopold Thun
he attempted in 1848 to open a music school in Prague.
It was a hardy enterprise, as his poverty was so great that
he could scarcely afford the hire of a piano for his own
practice. In this plight, as we have seen, he sought and
obtained help from Liszt. In 1849 he married Kateřina
Otilie, a girl whom he had met in the Pilsen days and who
had shared some of his musical studies.

The compositions of Smetana's early manhood fall into two groups. First, he provided his pupils with a great deal of practice and concert material, particularly in the form of arrangements and original works for four and eight hands. Secondly, he showed his awareness of current sentiments round about the year 1848 by writing a Students' March and a Solemn Overture. Both these pieces were a gesture of sympathy with the Slav movement that aimed at reviving and developing the Czech language, history, and other institutions. Bohemia was still officially under Austrian rule, and perhaps Smetana was apprehensive about the consequences if the authorities heard of his relations with the nationalist party. He seems to have attempted to assert his loyalty to the established order by dedicating his E major Symphony, whose Finale quotes the tune of Haydn's Emperor's Hymn, to Franz Josef I; and when the dedication was declined he felt it expedient to leave Bohemia for a time.

Between 1856 and 1861 he lived chiefly in Sweden. He conducted a musical society (*Sällskapet för Klassisk Sang*) at Göteborg, introducing to the Swedish public a number of important choral works, such as Mendelssohn's *St. Paul* and *Elijah*, Schumann's *Paradise and the Peri*, and parts of Wagner's *Tannhäuser* and *Lohengrin*. He kept in touch with Liszt, contributed two pieces to a collection under Liszt's editorship, and emulated his symphonic poems in *Richard III*, *Valdštýnův tábor* (*Wallenstein's Camp*), and *Haakon Jarl*. These works are almost devoid of the national colouring associated with Smetana's later music;

not so the piano pieces also produced at this time, and containing in the polkas especially some nostalgic memories of the land he had left. He was not, however, cut off altogether from Bohemia; he took holidays there from time to time, and brought over his wife to join him in Sweden. Unhappily the northern climate was fatal to her. In 1858 Smetana re-married. His second wife was Barbara Fernandini, and it was mainly owing to her homesickness that he resigned his post in Sweden and returned to Prague. By this time the political atmosphere was healthier for an artist of his stamp. The authorities had taken up a more liberal attitude, and Smetana found that his nationalist sympathies were no longer discouraged. He directed a choral society known as *Hlahol* ('Sound'), he helped to found a Czech Society of Artists (*Umělecká beseda*), and when, in 1862, a Provisional Theatre was inaugurated the way was open to him to found and foster a national school of opera.

The first of Smetana's operas on national subjects was *Branibori v Čechach* (The Brandenburgers in Bohemia). The most celebrated of the series, *Prodana Nevěsta* (The Bartered Bride), had a somewhat curious history. It was begun in 1863 and finished three years later in the form of a two-act *singspiel*, with spoken dialogue. A subsequent revision made it into a three-act opera, among the additional numbers being the popular *polka* and *furiant*. The third and final version, performed in 1874, contained recitative in place of the spoken dialogue. Smetana, unlike the great Russian composers of opera—Mussorgsky, Borodin, and Rimsky-Korsakov, was opposed to the use of actual folk-tunes in his works, and the melodic material of *The Bartered Bride* is entirely original. It is nevertheless saturated in Czech folk-music, not merely in the celebrated dance-movements—the *polka* and *furiant*—but also in the vigorous choruses, Czech counterparts of those in Bizet's *Carmen*, and in the solo and concerted numbers, such as the duets, with their sequences of languishing sixths, between Jenik and Mařenka, or the richly comic music allotted to Kecal the marriage-broker and the stuttering, half-witted Vašek.

Yet *The Bartered Bride* does not show us the full range of Smetana's genius. For other, more serious sides of it we must turn to *Dalibor*, one of the noblest classics of Czech music. It was first heard at the opening of the National Theatre in Prague on the 16th May 1868. The plot, which superficially resembles that of Beethoven's *Fidelio*, is founded on national legend, and gives splendid scope both for pageantry and for characterisation. The majestic theme that symbolises the hero and liberator, Dalibor, is used symphonically throughout the opera and the whole score is filled with magnificent sonority.

Another work of great national moment was *Libuše*, a kind of historical pageant dealing with the reign of a queen renowned in Czech history. The composer always insisted that this was not an opera for the repertory but should be used on special occasions. A great part of the action takes place in the Castle of Vysehrad, but the scenes on the homestead of Premysl, the peasant whom

Libuše chooses as her consort, provide opportunities for pastoral music in the vein of *The Bartered Bride*.

Smetana's later operas are still less known outside Czechoslovakia. *Dvě Vdovy* (The Two Widows), *Hubička* (The Kiss), and *Tajemství* (The Secret) all have excellent numbers, and paint the Bohemian countryside most charmingly. *Čertova Stěna* (The Devil's Wall) is founded on a weird legend of the Vltava.

A few months after the first production of *The Two Widows* in September 1874 Smetana disclosed to the directors of the National Theatre that he was doomed to complete deafness, and asked to be relieved of his duties as conductor at the Theatre. His hearing deteriorated with terrifying rapidity; he was obsessed by a high-pitched note sounding continually in his ears—an affliction realistically depicted in the last movement of the String Quartet in E minor (*From my Life*). With the onset of total deafness he retired into the Bohemian woods, from which the inspiration for so much of his music had come, and as the guest of his daughter Sophie and her husband, a forest ranger, he continued to compose works he could no longer hear.

One group of these works stands apart from his operas, and has passed into the standard orchestral repertory. This is the cycle of symphonic poems entitled *Ma Vlást* (My Country) and begun in 1874. It is made up of six pieces, each intended to evoke some aspect of Bohemian scenery, legend, or history. *Vyšehrad* takes its title from the ruined castle of Libuše standing high above the Vltava near Prague; it begins and ends with the ghostly harp-chords of Lunir, the minstrel. *Vltava*, the most popular of the set, is a musical panorama of the river itself. *Šárka* is based on the legend of a warrior queen and her vengeance on Ctirad, her wooer. *Z českých luhů a hájů* (From Bohemia's Woods) was the first of the series to be written in Smetana's woodland retreat, and is a song of thanksgiving for the beauty of the land of Bohemia. *Tábor* commemorates the castle founded by the Warriors of God, the followers of John Huss, and introduces a famous Hussite chorale. *Blaník* is the mountain where the heroes of the Hussite struggle sleep until their country's need shall again summon them forth.

Almost contemporary with the last of these symphonic poems are the Czech Dances, published, it is interesting to note, in 1877 after the appearance of the first set of Dvořák's Slavonic Dances.

The String Quartet, *From my Life*, has already been mentioned. According to the composer's own 'programme', the first movement is meant to convey his youthful enthusiasm and joy in his art; the second movement recalls, by its polka rhythm, his early fondness for dance music, and in the *meno vivo* section we are meant to catch a glimpse of the aristocratic circles, like that of Count Thun, where he sometimes moved; the third movement is a tender memory of his early love for Kateřina; the fourth movement begins with an allusion to his awakening to the possibilities of using national material in his compositions: but his delight in this discovery soon gives way to despair on realising the tragic end that awaits him. A reiterated, high-pitched violin 'E' reproduces the whistling in the ear that preceded Smetana's deafness. The second Quartet, in D minor, was written some six years after the first. Like *From my Life* it is to some extent autobiographical. As the composer explained, it begins where the first Quartet left off, with a catastrophe, and is in part an attempt to depict the confusion of ideas in the brain of a deaf man. From the purely musical aspect the D minor Quartet is of great interest, though its rhapsodical form and contrapuntal intricacy, so characteristic of Smetana's later works, make it a somewhat difficult work to follow.

On the 2nd March 1884 a concert was given in Prague in honour of Smetana's sixtieth birthday. He was unable to attend, for his general health had begun to deteriorate. He suffered from loss of breath, aphasia, and other distressing symptoms. He was forbidden to work, read, or even think about music. The preceding summer he had begun to work at an opera based on Shakespeare's *Twelfth Night* and entitled *Viola*, but there was now no hope of finishing it. A complete mental breakdown made it necessary for him to enter an asylum, and he died on the 12th May 1884. His grave is in the cemetery of Vyšehrad, the hallowed site of those vanished glories Smetana had recalled to the imagination of his countrymen.

BORODIN

THE life-story of Alexander Porphyrevich Borodin is a curious mixture of the romantic and the matter-of-fact. Born 12th November (N.S.) 1833 at Petersburg and reputed to have been the natural son of a Georgian prince, he spent the fifty-three years of his life not merely blamelessly, but in rendering to his fellow-men a variety of services, of which the composition of some excellent music formed only one part.

Like most of the other members of the Russian 'Five' Borodin was not encouraged in youth to think of music as a career. Instead, he was trained for the medical profession. At the same time, he was allowed to take lessons in cello and flute playing and to dabble in composition. An appointment to a military hospital at the age of twenty-two brought about a meeting with Mussorgsky, then a smartly dressed, elegantly accomplished young army officer, much in demand in drawing rooms. Two years later Borodin graduated as a Doctor of Medicine, and in 1859 set off on a three-years' tour of various European countries, primarily with the object of adding to his scientific knowledge, but also in the hope of hearing more music and meeting musical people. His scientific researches were carried out chiefly in Heidelberg and Paris; and his discoveries in the field of organic chemistry are said to have been of real importance.

On his return to Petersburg he married Katerina

Protopopova, a talented pianist he had met at Heidelberg. He settled down to a busy life as lecturer first at the Petersburg Medical Academy, and from 1864 onwards at the Military Academy, where he held a professorial appointment until his death. He had renewed his friendship with Mussorgsky, and was soon introduced to another member of the coterie, the brilliant pianist and enthusiast for folk-music, Balakirev. Under Balakirev's eye Borodin followed his musical studies more intensively, and as early as 1862 began his First Symphony, in E flat.

This work was not completed until seven years later, when Balakirev conducted the first performance and the influential critic Serov gave it his warm commendation. It contains, especially in the first and slow movements, and in the exciting Scherzo, much that is characteristic of Borodin at his best, but its initial popularity was soon to be surpassed by that of the brilliant Second Symphony.

The years 1869-1879 were from the musical point of view the most productive in Borodin's life, although his other interests also took heavy toll. He was engaged throughout this period not only in lecturing and writing scientific papers but also in carrying on propaganda for the extension of medical training to women. Among the smaller works he produced must be mentioned a number of songs, some of which, like *The Queen of the Sea* and *The Sleeping Princess* with their highly interesting piano accompaniments, in which consecutive seconds predominate, broke fresh harmonic ground and influenced the French Impressionists. At this same period he also made his first essays in writing opera. He first considered using as a libretto *The Tsar's Bride*, which was later to be composed by Rimsky-Korsakov. Then he took up the mediaeval epic of *Prince Igor*, worked on it for a time, and dropped it to write music for an opera-ballet, *Mlada*, another subject that was eventually to be realised in music by Rimsky-Korsakov.

In 1871 he returned with fresh zeal to *Prince Igor*, and in the years that remained to him brought it almost to the point of completion. After Borodin's death the score was finished mainly by Rimsky-Korsakov, who thus had a hand in the two greatest operas that have ever come out of Russia—*Prince Igor* and Mussorgsky's *Boris Godunov*. The celebrated Polovtsian Dances in Act II of *Prince Igor* and the *Polovtsian* March in Act III owe their barbaric instrumental colouring to Rimsky-Korsakov. The Overture, founded mainly on themes from the opera and often heard separately as a concert piece, was written down and scored by Glazunov from his recollections of hearing it played on the piano by the composer. But the credit remains with Borodin for creating one of the finest operatic works of the century. From the point of view of dramatic construction and characterisation it does not rank among the highest, but its range of expression is immense: from the poignant nobility of Yaroslavna's soliloquies to the drunken foolery of Yeroshka and Skula, from the primitive unaccompanied harmonies of the Choir of Villagers in Act IV to the quasi-oriental splendours of the Polovtsian music in Act II. Far more frankly and successfully than any of the German romantics, the Russians re-created the spirit of paganism, and in the opening of *Prince Igor*, as in that of *Boris Godunov* and Rimsky-Korsakov's *Snow-Maiden*, the worship of the Sun and other natural forces, and their identification with the human leader of the tribe or nation, is made to seem a credible reality rather than antiquarian make-believe. *Prince Igor* is impregnated with Russian folk-music, and yet owes allegiance to the traditions of Italian opera, especially in the prominence it gives to the human voice, in the song-like character of its melodies, and in the acceptance of the convention of self-contained 'numbers' which Wagner, at this period, was bent on destroying. Yet the orchestra has no mean part to play, and the various scenes are conceived symphonically; a good example of this occurs in Act I, when the girls come to Yaroslavna to ask for her protection. The 5/4 episode with its reiterated staccato notes and harmonic clashes recalls the scherzo of the Second Symphony. In the Polovtsian scenes the oriental side of Borodin's imagination comes into its own, and the languid, highly decorated phrases thrown out, for example, in Konchakovna's cavatina contrast powerfully with the more compact utterances of the 'Russian' scenes.

The Second Symphony in B minor was begun a year after Borodin had resumed work on *Prince Igor*. In its final form, as completed in 1876, it is probably the most satisfying of all Borodin's works and is now recognised as one of the most notable symphonies of its generation, thoroughly Russian in its rhythmic energy, passionate melodic outpouring, and harmonic richness, yet far better disciplined by the principles of classical form than the rather better known symphonies of Tchaikovsky. Its opening motif is as magnificently terse as that of Beethoven's Fifth Symphony. Borodin's unfinished Third Symphony may be mentioned here, although it belongs to a later stage in the composer's life. The scherzo, written in 5/8 time, achieves a most original and brilliant effect. After Borodin's death, Glazunov again came to the rescue and finished and scored these two movements.

The two String Quartets provide further evidence of Borodin's power of organising abstract music and at the same time giving it lyric warmth. The A major Quartet owed its original impetus to Beethoven's B flat Quartet (Op. 130), from which part of a theme is quoted in the first subject group of Borodin's first movement. The Quartet in D is a richly sonorous work. A bold use of the cello, as in the opening of the first and third movements gives it a fervent, glowing colour. A few minor chamber works call for mention. Borodin contributed a *Serenata alla spagnuola* to a String Quartet written iointly by Rimsky-Korsakov, Liadov, Borodin, and Glazunov as a tribute to Belaiev, their enlightened publisher, and founded on an adaptation of his name to musical notation (B=B flat; la=A; F). Another movement called forth by Belaiev's publishing activities was a collection of pieces for String Quartet written by various composers and entitled *Les Vendredis*. For this Borodin transcribed the 5/8 scherzo from his unfinished Third Symphony.

Yet a third example of the kind of communal pleasantry in which members of the 'Five' and their friends liked to indulge is the set of *Paraphrases* on the 'chopsticks' theme; in this Borodin joined Cui, Liadov, and Rimsky-Korsakov in providing ingenious harmonic and rhythmic patterns that can be played by one keyboard performer against the homely two-fingered ostinato of another (fsfs/mlml/rtrt/dd'dd'). One of Borodin's efforts is a little polka, to which Liszt deigned to write an introduction that is itself a variation.

Borodin had made a point of calling on Liszt during 1877, when he was in Germany. The Abbé received him with his usual warmth of interest in young visitors from abroad, and made him play with him four-hand versions of the two Symphonies and sing excerpts from *Prince Igor*. In acknowledgment of Liszt's kindness Borodin dedicated to him the short tone-poem, *In the Steppes of Central Asia*. This orchestral piece, though scarcely representative of Borodin at his best, has become popular through the simple and picturesque idea on which it is based—a caravan of Asiatic merchants, symbolised by an oriental melody, escorted by a guard of soldiers indicated by a folk-tune suggestive of European Russia. It is the pictorial setting of *Prince Igor* in miniature.

In August 1885 Borodin's travels reached as far as Belgium, where the Russian school had a vigorous patron in the Comtesse de Mercy-Argenteau. She supported at Liège three concerts of works by Russian composers, including Borodin's First Symphony, *In the Steppes of Central Asia*, and the *Petite Suite* for piano, which was dedicated to her. In the winter of the same year Borodin was again in Belgium, this time in company with César Cui. Not only did Borodin hear his Second Symphony played in Brussels but he and Cui had the satisfaction of seeing the windows of Belgian music-dealers filled with their own scores and those of Rimsky-Korsakov and Glazunov.

Less than a year after his return to Russia, Borodin fell seriously ill. On the 28th February 1887 he died suddenly in his fifty-fourth year. His grave is beside Mussorgsky's in the Alexander Nevsky cemetery and his monument records the two dominant interests of his life in a pair of emblems—part of a musical score and the symbols of a chemical formula. Of the value of Borodin's contribution to music there can be no measure; his output may seem small beside that of a Brahms or a Dvořák, but such was the concentration of intellect and emotion he was able to produce in the precious hours he could devote to composition that there is little that is not pure gold.

RIMSKY-KORSAKOV

A NOTORIOUS film has embroidered the early life-story of Nicolas Rimsky-Korsakov into a fantasy so absurd that it might have been thought too much even for a generation conditioned to the inanities of celluloid biography. Yet the plain facts of his career contain an element of the incalculable, if not of the miraculous; and his artistic personality shows a preoccupation with fantastic subject-matter, with crude, brilliant colour, and with an almost hypnotic glitter of surface-effect that entitle him to be regarded as the wizard among Russian composers—or more aptly, perhaps, as a strange, not altogether tangible personage like the Astrologer in his own opera, *The Golden Cockerel.*

As with other members of the 'Five', music was not originally chosen as his profession. His grandfather had been an admiral in the Russian navy, his elder brother had followed the same calling, and he himself felt strongly attracted to the sea from an early age. He was born in 1844, twenty-two years after his brother Voin, the sailor; this discrepancy of ages doubtless added a spice of hero-worship to Nicolas's ambition to enter the Navy. Of musical talent he showed unmistakable signs in childhood. Music was cultivated in the home with some enthusiasm, but little depth or discernment, and the boy's first lessons in piano-playing do not seem to have carried him far. More important were the fragments of Russian folk song

he picked up from members of the family, including his
mother, who was of peasant stock.

In 1856 Nicolas became a naval cadet at Petersburg.
Residence in the capital gave him more opportunities of
hearing good music; and, characteristically it was opera
that first fired his imagination. Besides the works of the
German romantic school he came across those of Glinka,
and found them strangely fascinating. He was encouraged
in his admiration for Glinka by F. A. Canille, with whom
he had begun to take lessons and who introduced him to
three contemporary Russian composers, all members of
the 'Five': Balakirev, Cui, and Mussorgsky. Of the three
it was Balakirev, the brilliant pianist and collector of folk
songs, who influenced him most strongly. The attraction
was mutual; Balakirev realised the extraordinary gifts
latent in the young man and he helped to initiate him
into the mysteries of orchestration.

According to Rimsky-Korsakov's own account, his musical knowledge was still fragmentary. Even Balakirev's
teaching had not availed to piece it together. He played
the piano erratically, he had no idea of the names or functions of the chords he was discovering empirically and
using in his attempts at composition, and he knew little
of the technique of orchestral instruments. His new
friends, except Mussorgsky, whose technical equipment
was also in an experimental state, did their best to help
him; but his studies were again to be interrupted. In
April 1862 he passed out of the Naval College, was
appointed to the clipper 'Almaz', and later that year

sailed in her for England, the first stage of a long cruise.

During the four months the 'Almaz' lay at Gravesend for repairs Rimsky-Korsakov and some of his fellow-officers explored London and improved their general education by much reading and discussion. Rimsky-Korsakov also worked on an ambitious project he had begun under Balakirev—the composition of a Symphony in E flat minor. As may be imagined, this work made slow progress.

After a period of duty in Russian waters, the 'Almaz' was ordered across the Atlantic, and lay for some months off the coast of America awaiting a possible outbreak of war between Russia and Britain. In the Spring of 1864 the ship was recalled. Part of the homeward course lay through the Southern Atlantic, where Rimsky-Korsakov had his first experience of the beauty of tropical seas—an experience that may have inspired some of the iridescent scoring of *Sheherazade*.

On his return to Petersburg, Rimsky-Korsakov renewed his contacts with Balakirev and other members of the 'Five', and under the spur of Balakirev's encouragement completed his Symphony and wrote several songs, the Overture on Russian Themes, and the tone-poem *Sadko*. Although the sea was still nominally his profession his duties had become, for the time being, of the lightest; such were the privileges of the officer classes in Tsarist Russia. On the other hand, he was being drawn more and more into the society of musicians, including not only those already named but also Dargomizhky, composer of the much-discussed opera, *The Stone Guest*, which Rimsky-Korsakov was eventually to score after the composer's death in 1869. Rimsky-Korsakov's friends had discovered in him a natural flair for instrumentation, and he found large-scale works taking shape in his mind. The Symphonic Suite *Antar* has a programmatic basis. In the first movement Antar receives from the Queen of Palmyra the promise of 'the three joys of life', symbolised by a musical theme. In the remaining three movements the 'joys'—revenge, power, and love—are represented by transformations of the same theme. Another important work, *The Maid of Pskov*, was being written during the winter of 1871, when Rimsky-Korsakov was sharing an apartment with Mussorgsky, who also was engaged on an opera—*Boris Godunov*.

It was at this comparatively early stage in his career as a serious musician that Rimsky-Korsakov accepted the post of professor of composition in the Petersburg Conservatory. On his own confession he lacked knowledge of every branch of text-book musicianship; the successes he had already achieved were the result of innate musical gifts of a high order and of an unusual capacity for gaining and applying practical experience, but he lacked even a systematic vocabulary of technical language in which to expound his art to students. Yet his quickness of wit and zest for hard work enabled him from the first to keep ahead of his pupils and eventually to grow into an erudite as well as an inspiring teacher. His marriage to Nadezhda Purgold, a sensitive and highly-trained musician, also contributed towards the strengthening of his technical equipment. An ally of another kind was Krabbe, the Minister of Marine, who smoothed his path through the labyrinth of intrigue and official vetoes surrounding the production of an opera by a Russian composer, and secured him an appointment as Inspector of Naval Bands that gave him first-hand experience of wind instruments. Soon afterwards he took on yet another official responsibility, that of Director of the Free School of Music.

All this time he was toiling at student's 'paper-work'— harmony, counterpoint, fugue, and orchestration—and his exercises overflowed into his free composition to such a degree that he began to gain the reputation of being an academician, much to the disappointment of his more radically nationalist friends. That he had not lost his interest in national music was shown, however, by the *Collection of One Hundred Russian Folk-songs* which he made partly from oral traditions current in his own family, and harmonised during 1876 and 1877; and also by his unflagging study of Glinka's scores, which inspired him to further attempts in the field of opera. He revised *The Maid of Pskov*—not for the last time; like Liszt, he rarely remained content with his works in their original form, and not only *The Maid of Pskov* but also *Sadko*, *Antar*, and the *First Symphony* were thus treated. His next two important works were also operas: *May Night*, based on a story of Gogol's, and *The Snow Maiden*. The latter was written, mainly in 1880, during a wonderful summer spent on a large estate, where the peace and luxuriance of nature seemed to breathe the spirit of the old Slav nature-myths that Rimsky-Korsakov had already met with in Russian folk-song.

After the production of *The Snow Maiden* there came a gap in his creative life. Between 1882 and 1887 he wrote little. He dropped two of his official appointments, those of Inspector of Marine Bands and Director of the Free School, and took up another, as assistant to Balakirev in directing the music in the Imperial Chapel. He had lost one of his old friends in Mussorgsky, who died in 1881, and now had the task of revising and orchestrating Mussorgsky's unfinished compositions. Six years later, as we have seen, he had to perform a similar service on behalf of Borodin. He was now at the height of his mastery of the orchestra. Recently there has been a strong reaction against his alterations to the original versions of *Boris Godunov*—the composer himself left more than one—but it is impossible to withhold admiration for the brilliant colouring he often superimposed on other men's outlines and textures. The barbaric splendours of the Polovtsian Dances owe almost as much to him as to Borodin.

Three original works of the period 1887-8 indicate a fresh flow of ideas. All have passed into the orchestral concert repertory and on them is based much of the composer's popularity. They illustrate his ability to put together a vivid score, to pile one sensuous climax on another, and to pour out an unfailing flood of attractive, if somewhat artificial, melody with just the right amount of exotic character to titillate the average western listener. Like Elgar, he gets orchestral players on to his side by writing effectively for the instruments, so that it is not an unusual experience to hear his music really well performed. In the *Spanish Capriccio* he builds up a tourist's impression of Spanish costumes and dances—an effect that Russian composers had sought after from Glinka onwards. In the *Easter Overture* it is the liturgy of the Russian church and its external trappings of bells and vestments that forms the subject of his panorama. In *Sheherazade* it is a pseudo-oriental colouring, found also in other works: *Antar*, for example, and *Sadko* and *The Golden Cockerel*.

The three years following this brilliantly successful group of works were clouded with personal tragedy and disillusionment. Two of the composer's children died, and he himself suffered from a physical and mental lassitude that rendered him incapable of writing, though he attempted to stimulate his imagination by studying aesthetics, philosophy and related subjects. The one important work of the period is the opera *Mlada*. His temperament, however, was a resilient one and by 1894 he felt his vitality returning. With *Christmas Eve* and *Sadko* (to be distinguished from his earlier tone poem with the same title) he began a new series of operas that included some little known outside Russia: *Mozart and Salieri*, *The Tsar's Bride*, *Tsar Saltan* (even more prolific than usual in wonders, including the famous bumble-bee episode), *Servilia*, *Kashchey the Immortal*, and *Kitezh*.

In 1905, as a consequence of his upholding some pro-revolutionary conduct of his Conservatory students, Rimsky-Korsakov came into conflict with political authority. The Conservatory was closed, the Director and some of his staff were dismissed, and Rimsky-Korsakov retired to the country to finish his great text-book on instrumentation (illustrated almost entirely by examples from his own scores) and his bulky volume of memoirs. Glazunov was appointed to the Conservatory in his place; and Rimsky-Korsakov spent some of his increased leisure on a new opera, *The Golden Cockerel*. In spite of a number of interruptions, including a trip of Paris to conduct concerts of Russian music under the auspices of Diaghilev, the opera was finished in the summer of 1906. It was his last work. During the early months of 1908 he began to suffer from heart trouble, and on the 21st June he died. He left behind a mass of correspondence and autobiographical material, much of which is available in his *Annals of my Musical Life*, edited and enlarged by his son Andrey.

GRIEG

IN 1814 Norway, having existed for hundreds of years as a dependency of Denmark, broke away and drew up for herself one of the earliest, and as events were to show, one of the most durable democratic constitutions on the Continent. Pride in this hardly-won independence was further stimulated by the effects of the romantic movement in literature and art, which led the educated classes to realise the beauty to be found in the traditional lore, folk-music, and handicrafts of the peasantry and fishermen.

Knowledge of such things penetrated slowly, however, to the mercantile, professional, and official families who even as late as 1843, when Edvard Grieg was born in the home of the English Consul at Bergen, remained predominantly Danish in language and cultural sympathies. It is doubtful if Edvard ever heard his mother, an accomplished musician, play or sing a genuine Norwegian folk-tune; on the other hand, he heard a great deal of Mozart, Beethoven, Weber, and Chopin. Under his mother's teaching he made such progress in piano playing and extemporisation as to attract the notice of the famous violinist Ole Bull, who settled near the Griegs and paid them a visit when Edvard was about fifteen. He urged them to send their gifted son to Leipzig, whose Conservatory of Music, founded by Mendelssohn and Schumann in the year of Edvard's birth, had become the goal of students from all over Europe.

Grieg was registered at the Conservatory in 1859. His shy and sensitive disposition made him react against un-inspired, mechanical teaching, such as he was unfortunate enough to receive from some of the Conservatory staff, But there were compensations; in Wenzel, the friend of Schumann, and in Moritz Hauptmann at least he found sympathetic guides, and there were the Gewandhaus con-certs, at which he heard Clara Schumann play her hus-band's Piano Concerto, and the opera house, where he attended performance after performance of *Tannhäuser*. In spite of a breakdown in health that left him a lifelong sufferer from chest troubles he managed to acquire a sound piano technique and a fluent command of contemporary German harmonic idiom. Among his earliest published works were a set of songs to German words and some piano pieces in the Schumann-Mendelssohn tradition, both written in his student days.

Grieg returned to Norway with an excellent report from the Conservatory in his pocket. The musical public of Bergen was proud of him and supported the series of re-citals with which he opened his professional career. But neither Bergen nor Christiania in those days could give a young artist the stimulus he needed, and before long he found an opportunity to spend several months in Cop-enhagen, where lived and worked leaders of the Danish romantic school like H. C. Andersen, author of the fairy tales and of some delicate lyric poetry, and the composers J. P. E. Hartmann and Niels Gade. As a diligent and respected, though rarely inspired, writer of symphonies overtures, cantatas, and chamber music, Gade was not impressed by the young Norwegian's slender output and urged him to attempt something on a larger scale. The outcome of this advice was a symphony which Grieg, against his natural inclination, completed and subsequently abandoned, though the two middle movements were printed as detached pieces for piano duet (Op. 14). More fertile in artistic results were his meeting with H. C. Andersen, some of whose verses Grieg set under the titles of *Melodies of the Heart* (Op. 5). This collection included 'Two brown eyes' and 'I love thee', the latter Grieg's most popular though by no means his best song.

Two more friendships that Grieg formed in Copenhagen were to alter the whole course of his life and career. The first was with his cousin, Nina Hagerup, who had been brought up in Denmark and trained as a singer. She married Grieg on the 11th June 1867. The other was with Rikard Nordraak, a young and ambitious composer who had written incidental music for plays by the Norwegian dramatist Bjørnson and who communicated to Grieg his own impetuous enthusiasm for anything that could be called 'Norwegian' in melody, rhythm, or harmony. Whether he introduced Grieg to any actual folksongs is doubtful; but it was he who confirmed Grieg in the determination to cultivate a national idiom and seek inspiration in the legendary and historical lore of Norway. A proof that the influence of Leipzig was not to be shed without a period of compromise is given in the conventional title, *Four Humoresques* (Op. 6) which masks the set of Scandinavian dances written soon after Grieg's first encounter with Nordraak and dedicated to him. Very much the same is true of the two Sonatas, one for piano (Op. 7) and the other for violin and piano (Op. 8) in F, the first of Grieg's three sonatas for this combination, in both of which we watch him trying to pour the new wine of folk-idioms into the old bottles of classical form. These two sonatas were written in Denmark in the summer of 1865. The Piano Sonata in particular seems to owe much to Gade's own Piano Sonata in the same key (E minor). One more work must be mentioned as belonging to Grieg's transitional period. It is the Concert Overture, *In Autumn* (Op. 11) based on Grieg's song *Autumn Storm* and written during a holiday in Rome in the winter of 1865-6. At this time also Grieg received news of Nordraak's death from consumption and paid tribute to his friend in the poignant *Funeral March*. In Rome he met his most distinguished countryman, Henrik Ibsen, who was then living in exile. Ibsen encouraged Grieg to apply to Bjørnson for the post of musical director at the National Theatre in Christiania. But another candidate was appointed and after considering the idea of becoming a church organist Grieg returned to Norway to continue in Christiania his career as pianist, conductor, teacher, and, as far as time should allow, as composer. Standards of performance in choral and orchestral music were not high in Norway in those days and Grieg worked hard to raise them and to extend the repertory. In intervals of leisure that occurred in the summer months he produced the first set of the *Lyric Pieces* for piano and, again during a summer holiday in Denmark, the A minor Concerto for piano and orchestra (Op. 16), a work that like many others underwent revision and rescoring in later years. One of the first people to read through the Concerto in manuscript was Liszt, who had written to Grieg towards the end of 1868, spontaneously and generously commending some of his earlier work and inviting him to pay a visit to Weimar. The meeting eventually took place in Rome about a year later. The Cantata *At a Southern Convent's Gate* was dedicated to Liszt. Grieg wrote it to a text by Bjørnson, a most prolific poet, prose writer, and dramatist, and a man capable of friendship on a generous scale. In the next few years he and Grieg collaborated in several works, including the melodrama *Bergliot*, the cantata *Landsighting*, incidental music to *Sigurd the Crusader*, and a number of songs whose texts were taken mainly from Bjørnson's stories of peasant life. An opera, *Olav Trygvason*, also was planned, but progressed no further than the first three scenes.

In the meantime the other Norwegian literary giant of the day, Ibsen, had commissioned Grieg to write incidental music for his poetical drama *Peer Gynt*, which was about to be produced for the first time on the stage. Altogether Grieg wrote about two dozen pieces in response to this request, including songs, dance-tunes, preludes, entractes, and melodramatic settings. Eight of these movements, collected into the two *Peer Gynt* Suites, did more than any of his larger works, except the Piano Concerto, to advance his reputation abroad. The complete *Peer Gynt* with Grieg's music was first performed at Christiania on the 24th February 1876. In the same year Grieg composed the Op. 25 songs to lyrics by Ibsen, including 'A Swan' and 'To a Water-lily'.

Summer months spent beside the fjords of Western Norway, and a study of the great collection of folk-music made by O. M. Lindeman, helped Grieg to get into closer touch with genuine folk song. He arranged some of Lindeman's tunes for piano and for male voice chorus, and wrote the G minor String Quartet (Op. 27) which is impregnated with folk-tune influences. The *Ballade* for piano (Op. 24) is also founded on a folk-song. Grieg finally sealed his allegiance to the scenery and traditions of the lovely Hardanger region by building the villa Troldhaugen; it was ready in the spring of 1885 and remained the Griegs' permanent home up to the last few months of the composer's life.

There were, however, many periods of absence from Troldhaugen. The fresh and delicate charm of Grieg's work and the novelty of its harmonic and rhythmic style had begun to earn him an international reputation and, he was continually in demand as player and conductor of his own works. His wife shared many of his triumphs, for her interpretations of his songs, now recognised as containing much of his best music, were unsurpassed for sensitive artistry. As the years went by Grieg rarely attempted to compose a large-scale work, though the popularity of the Piano Concerto and of the Sonatas made it necessary for him to take part in many performances of them. He turned more and more to the piano miniature and to song-writing, and it was in those mediums that his individuality came to show itself most strongly. His settings of Bjørnson and Ibsen have already been mentioned. These poets wrote in the Riksmaal or Dano-Norwegian literary language, which differed considerably from the dialects spoken in various parts of Norway. A movement to base on the latter a common 'Loamshire' spoken and written literature was sponsored by a number of prose and verse writers, including A. O. Vinje and Arne Garborg, and Grieg composed some of his finest songs to poems by these two writers in the new Landsmaal or 'country speech'. The two books of Vinje Songs (Op. 33) were completed in the spring of 1880 and contain deeply-felt songs like 'The Spring' and 'The Wounded One' which the composer transcribed for strings under the title *Elegiac Melodies*. The lyrics from Garborg's *Haugtussa* belong to the next decade (Op. 67, 1895-8). In them Grieg reaches his highwatermark as a song-writer though difficulties of translation have caused them to be less widely known than the earlier songs.

It became Grieg's custom to spend some weeks of every summer walking or driving in the mountains, generally in company with friends, among whom he counted Frederick Delius and Percy Grainger. Delius was considerably influenced by Grieg's harmonic idiom, and Grainger made a special study of Grieg's keyboard music and was particularly happy in his readings of the *Slåtter*, or Nor-

E

wegian fiddle tunes, which Grieg arranged from transcriptions Johan Halvorsen had noted down from the playing of one of the last of the traditional fiddlers. Among
the mountain homesteads Grieg was able to hear for himself some of the living tradition of folk-music. Some of
his discoveries were recorded in his arrangements for
piano, the *Norwegian Folk Melodies* (Op. 66).

Grieg died on the 4th September 1907, on the eve of a
visit to England to conduct at the Leeds Festival. His last
published work was *Four Psalms* (Op. 74), a set of choral
arrangements of tunes and words current in the Norwegian
Church since the Reformation. They are typical of the
last period of the composer's work, which includes the
songs and piano pieces mentioned in the preceding para-
graphs and also some of the later *Lyric Pieces*, like the remarkable *Klokkeklang* (*Bell-ringing*, Op. 54, No. 6). These
are at once the most original and the least known of his
compositions. They have a more astringent flavour than
some of his more popular early works, and in their time
they were regarded as 'advanced'. Among those who
found them of special interest were the younger French
composers of the impressionist school. Debussy was personally hostile to Grieg, but nevertheless absorbed a number of his ideas; Ravel openly and gratefully acknowledged
his influence.

FRANCK

IT is common enough in bilingual Belgium for a child to bear a Flemish surname and a French baptismal name. That César Franck should have done so may be considered symbolical. In his contrapuntal ingenuity and fondness for massive tonal effects he shows traits of mind that we associate with the Netherlands composers of the fifteenth and sixteenth centuries. On the other hand, although he was born (on the 10th December 1822) at Liège he spent the greater part of his life in Paris, and is rightly considered to be one of the founders of modern French music.

His father, a banker, soon discovered the unusual talent that César shared with his younger brother Joseph and resolved to make them both keyboard virtuosi after the order of Thalberg and Liszt. Before he was twelve César had taken a course of lessons at the Liège Conservatory and had toured Belgium as an infant prodigy. He was then taken to Paris and became a pupil of the veteran flautist and composition teacher Anton Reicha. It may have been Reicha who gave the boy a lifelong affection for eighteenth century opera composers like Dalayrac, Grétry, Monsigny, and Méhul. Soon after Franck became his pupil Reicha died, and Franck was then, at the age of sixteen, admitted to the Paris Conservatoire. There his keyboard facility won him honours, though the venerable Director, Cherubini, was perturbed when César, to demonstrate his confidence at a sight-reading test, played the set passage faultlessly while transposing down a third. A year or so later, having taken up the organ, he confounded his examiners again by combining two different themes set for separate extemporisations.

The seemingly inevitable goal for such a student was the Prix de Rome, which would have allowed him to fulfil his private ambition to develop as a serious composer. But César's father still dreamt of seeing his son lionised in the salons and concert-halls of Europe, and for the time being his wishes had to be respected. Franck left the Conservatoire in 1842, before completing his normal course, returned to Belgium, and resigned himself to giving recitals, taking pupils, and composing for the piano showy operatic fantasias and similar pieces, including variations for piano duet on 'God save the Queen'. Of more durable quality were the four Trios for violin, cello and piano published in 1842-3. the first of these—Franck's Op. 1—is remarkable in that it carries out methodically the principle of theme-transformation and the practice of binding together the various movements of a work with a 'motto-theme', both well-known elements in the construction of his later works.

After a few years it was realised that Paris would offer a wider field both for César and for Joseph, and the young men established themselves as organists in the capital. César lived and worked from the first according to a definite plan, rising early to devote the first two hours of the day to composition, then running about Paris to give lessons at schools or private houses. In 1848, in the midst

of the February Revolution, he married Félicité Desmous-
seaux, one of his pupils and a member of a family well-
known in the acting profession. Three years later he was
appointed organist at St. Jean-Saint-François, and in 1858
he was invited to become principal organist at Ste. Clothilde, where a fine new Cavaillé-Coll organ had recently
been installed. This post he was to hold with great distinction during the next thirty-five years.

The period 1858-70 was occupied mainly in church
duties, including the composition of service music in the
saccharinic style of the day, in the endless round of teaching, and in giving occasional recitals. It was, in fact, not
unlike the way Elgar spent his life between the ages of
twenty and forty. Of the works written by Franck at this
time it is chiefly the organ pieces that have survived changes of fashion and taste, the *Six pièces pour grand orgue*
(Op. 16-21), composed at various times between 1862 and
1865 and showing not only Franck's accomplishment as
an organist but also his favourite methods of construction.
No. 3 is the popular *Prélude, fugue, et variation* afterwards
arranged by the composer for piano and harmonium, and
nowadays frequently heard as a piano solo. No. 4, the
Pastorale, is the father of many of the lighter movements
of modern organ literature; it is clearly related to passages
in Franck's oratorio *Ruth*, written in 1845 and performed
at the beginning of the following year—one of the few
resounding successes of his career.

The Franco-German War of 1870 brought great changes in the artistic outlook of the French people. Military

defeat was followed by a determination to resist Prussian influence in the field of ideas and to build up a body of French art that should command respectful attention throughout the civilised world. Paradoxically, the influence of German or German-trained composers played an important part in this renaissance. The instrumental works of Beethoven in particular were ardently studied, and a whole school of French composers led by Franck (and later his pupil d'Indy) and Saint-Saëns devoted itself to the production of serious chamber and orchestral music.

Franck's immediate personal reaction to the war had been to take out papers of nationalisation. Thereafter he emerged from the seclusion of his classroom and organ-loft and took a prominent part in fostering the new tendencies just described. In 1872, rather to his own surprise, for he had always been coldly treated by most of his academic contemporaries, he was appointed organ professor at the Conservatoire. He also became one of the most energetic members of the *Société nationale*, founded in 1871 by Saint-Saëns and Romaine Bussine to promote the composition and performance of works by native composers, whether experienced or unknown. Its motto was *Ars gallica*, and the spirit of chauvinism that actuated it may be traced down to Debussy's uncompromising attitude during the 1914-18 war. Most of Franck's later works were first produced at concerts of the Société.

Although two oratorios, *Les Béatitudes* and *La Rédemption*, and two operas, *Hulda* and *Ghisèle*, took up much of his time during the 70's, Franck's final period of creativeness was concerned mainly with orchestral and chamber music. Of the latter, the earliest and in many ways the most satisfying specimen was the Quintet in F minor for piano and strings (1878-9), where he carried out with fine artistry his principle of unification through the use of themes that are transformed, from movement to movement, according to the prevailing mood and atmosphere. The effectiveness of the Quintet is rivalled by that of the Sonata for violin and piano (1886), in the last movement of which the old device of canon is used both skilfully and freshly. The String Quartet in D is less often performed than either of the two foregoing works. Franck himself loved it and spent many hours in polishing it, and oddly enough it received praise from critics who had previously found little to commend in his music. But the romantic luxuriance of its texture is fatiguing to the ear of the modern listener who requires from chamber music above all things clean line-drawing and concise expression.

Among the chamber music must be counted the two great triptyches for piano solo: the *Prélude, chorale et fugue* (1884) and the *Prélude, aria et final* (1886-7). In these Franck's avowed intention was to adapt the older forms of variation, fugue, and sonata to his own cyclic plan, and to employ the resources of Lisztian piano technique. In carrying out this aim his early training as a concert pianist was of course a valuable aid.

He had also experimented with the piano as an orchestral instrument in his symphonic poem *Les Djinns* (1884), and contemporary with the triptych solo works for piano is the beautiful quasi-concerto *Variations symphoniques* (1885) for piano and orchestra, where the traditional plan of variations on a theme is used with much originality, one variation overlapping another and the thematic material developing organically. Theme-transformation and the 'motto-theme' are found again in the D minor Symphony. The slow movement of this work scandalised some of Franck's more conservative colleagues, partly because it made use of the cor anglais, an instrument hitherto regarded as having no standing outside the opera house, and partly because of the telescoping of allegretto and scherzo sections into a single movement. Minor orchestral works that still figure in concert programmes are the programmatic tone-poem *Le chasseur maudit* (1882) and the suite *Psyché*, which has choral episodes.

Franck had not ceased to play and compose for his organ. At the very close of his life he wrote down what we may imagine to be fairly faithful reproductions of his extemporisation at its best. The *Trois chorals* (1890) are not chorale preludes in the German tradition of Bach or Brahms, but are based on hymn-like themes of the composer's own, which are developed freely, varied, interwoven with subsidiary melodies, and relieved by episodes. This treatment owes something to Bach, but is nevertheless individual and romantic in the nineteenth century neo-Gothic style. Most popular of the *Chorals* is No. 3 in A minor. No 2, in B minor, exploits the old variation form of the passacaglia.

Franck died in the year these elaborate and deeply-felt works were published. Honours had at last come upon him, both in the form of official tributes and also in the reverence with which his pupils gathered round him. They included Duparc, Ropartz, Bordes, Lekeu, Chausson, and d'Indy, Franck's devoted biographer and chief apostle.

SAINT-SAËNS

CAMILLE SAINT-SAËNS has suffered a fate in some respects similar to that of his contemporary and idol, Franz Liszt. His fundamental seriousness of purpose, vast erudition, and tireless and often public-spirited industry are discredited, while attention is constantly drawn to the shallowness and lack of consistent taste and style that mar so much of his work. The schoolboy definition of a vacuum as a large empty space where the Pope lives might fairly be applied as it stands to the average musician's conception of Saint-Saëns and his music, the more so as his position in French musical life came to have much about it that was pontifical. Long before he reached his privileged eighties he had grown into a character, striking in appearance—'like a parrot', according to Pierre Lalo, formidable in conversation, and unpredictable in behaviour. His virtuosity on organ and piano, his feats of score-reading which so much astonished Liszt and Wagner, his prodigious memory of music and of books were a byword. The scope of his talent was remarkable. He won success not only in the opera-house but also in fields few of his countrymen had ventured into before him—the fields of symphony, symphonic poem, and chamber music. Yet his doctrinaire classicism was offset by a flair for the picturesque, a gift of lyrical fluency, and the inimitable Gallic ability to fashion music for pure entertainment and carry it off with a light and sure touch. With the delicious

Carnaval des animaux in our ears we can forgive Saint-Saëns for the *Africa* Suite and the *Danse macabre*, and perhaps we can even bring ourselves to forgive our fathers who induced him to write *The Promised Land* for the Three Choirs Festival of 1913.

Facility, the fatal gift of the gods to men like Saint-Saëns, generally reveals itself in extreme precocity. With Saint-Saëns, however, there was also a firm basis of technical discipline. He was born in Paris on the 9th October 1835, was playing the piano quite competently at the age of three; at five, in Gounod's words, 'il manquait déjà d'inexpérience'; he gave mature piano recitals at eleven, and at thirteen entered the Paris Conservatoire, where he studied the organ with Benoist and composition with Halévy. Although he failed, like several other notable French composers, to gain the highly-esteemed Prix de Rome, he was awarded in 1852 a special composition prize by the Société Ste. Cécile. In the same year he was appointed to his first important organ post, at the church of St. Merry. Six years later he became organist at the Madeleine, where he was to remain for nearly twenty years. In 1861 he began his influential career as professor at the École Niedermeyer; he held this appointment for three years only, but during that time he taught a number of gifted pupils, including Fauré, Messager, and Gigout.

In the meantime his own compositions were making headway. His first important success had occurred when the Société Ste. Cécile had performed his first Symphony, in E flat, in 1853. Three more Symphonies followed during the next six years; only the last of these was published, and has thus become known as the composer's Second Symphony, in A minor. It was about this time also that he began to produce the series of concertos—five for piano, three for violin, and two for cello—in which his talent for brilliance had full scope. The five for piano and orchestra provide a useful compendium of his development, if that word can be used of so eclectic a composer, and illustrate his technical accomplishment, his avid search for novel effects, and his failure to weld the elements he derived from various sources into a convincing personal idiom. Thus, the popular Second Concerto in G minor begins almost as if parodying a Bach toccata, continues with a theme suggestive of the mild romanticism of Mendelssohn, and covers the mixture with banal decoration in the manner of Liszt. The second movement, with its kettle-drum solo and clever adaptation of the fairyland scherzo of Berlioz and Mendelssohn, is more consistent and attractive. The finale is a tarantella of unabashed vulgarity. In the Third Concerto we have a commonplace first movement, a slow movement with touches of Franck's poetry, and a finale evoking the ballroom polka of the day. These comparatively early concertos (written in 1868 and 1869) may be placed for contrast beside the Fifth Concerto, which belongs to 1896 and shows the sixty-year old composer struggling harder than ever to keep up to date, and not to be outdone by younger contemporaries like Satie and Debussy, Fauré and Ravel. Thus there are impressionistic sequences of chords in root position, quasi-modal tonalities, experiments in pianistic overtones, plenty of diatonic sevenths, and in the second movement some oriental rhythms and a Nile boat-song 'collected' by Saint-Saëns on one of his holidays in the Orient.

We have already noticed, in dealing with the work of César Franck, that Saint-Saëns was among the leaders of the French musical renaissance that came about after 1870, and that he helped to found the *Société nationale de musique*. One of the aims of the *Société* was to build up an imposing body of contemporary French instrumental music, and in this field Saint-Saëns set an impressive example. Historically considered, his most influential contribution lay in the Symphonic Poems he produced in emulation of Liszt. *Le rouet d'Omphale* (1871) marks the introduction of this form into French music. It was followed by *Phaëton* (1873), *La danse macabre* (1874), which was transcribed—and glorified—for piano by Liszt and subsequently caricatured by the composer himself among the 'fossils' of *Le carnaval des animaux*, and *La jeunesse d'Hercule* (1877).

Another important section of his instrumental output was associated with the foundation, about 1860, of a chamber music society by an amateur named Lemoine. The extraordinary name of the society, *La Trompette*, accounts for the composition of Saint-Saëns' Septet for trumpet, string quartet, double bass and piano, an unusual combination treated, especially in the Gavotte, with deft spontaneity, and likewise of Vincent d'Indy's Suite for trumpet, two flutes, and strings. The Saint-Saëns work was published in 1881. The still better-known Suite, *Le carnaval des animaux*, was also written for *La Trompette*. It is essentially chamber music, adding flute, clarinet, celeste, and two pianos to a quartet of solo strings with double bass. Its brilliant allusiveness, combined with charming touches of musicianship and the most delicate scoring, give it a place almost to itself in musical literature; only, perhaps, in Walton's *Façade* Suites can we find something like a parallel. Everyone remembers the Elephant dancing to bits of Berlioz and Mendelssohn, and the Tortoise adapting an Offenbach cancan to his own pace, and the Fossils which are petrified popular tunes; side by side with these are delicious miniatures—the Aviary, the Aquarium, and the Swan. More conventional chamber works include a Piano Quintet, written as early as 1855, two Piano Trios, two String Quartets, a Piano Quartet, two Sonatas for violin and piano, and two for cello and piano. In these the academic side of the composer's personality is uppermost; wanting the passionate earnestness of Franck or the stylistic individuality of Fauré he falls back, when wit is out of place, on formal methods of construction and pattern-making. All the same, these works have a clarity of texture to which Fauré paid loyal and unstinted tribute.

For the same reasons that have driven his chamber music out of favour, Saint-Saëns no longer holds his own as a symphonist. The only work in this category that gets an occasional hearing is the Third Symphony (really his fifth) in C minor, which was written for the Philharmonic Society, dedicated to Liszt, and first performed in London in 1886. The originality of its plan—it is divided into two large sections—and the ingenuity of its theme-transformations command a certain intellectual homage, balanced by the sensuous effect of the tonal forces employed: a fairly large orchestra is supplemented with the organ and with a piano played duet-fashion. The whole constitutes a *tour de force* highly characteristic of the composer, though there are moments when one is reminded that Saint-Saëns stands in close, if degenerate, succession to Berlioz.

Zealous though he was in composing in purely instrumental forms, Saint-Saëns by no means neglected the stage. Only one of his operas, *Samson et Dalila*, is more than a name outside France. Its history is curious. Frustrated by the intrigues of the Parisian operatic world, Saint-Saëns was encouraged by Liszt to finish *Samson* and send it to Weimar, where its first production, under Liszt, took place in 1877. Censorship restrictions on the use of a Biblical subject prevented it from being presented on the French stage until 1890, and the still more scrupulous Covent Garden banned it until 1909. In the meantime, however, the English choral societies had adopted the voluptuous score as a sacred oratorio, giving it an unforeseen respectability by association with Handel, Mendelssohn, and Gounod. Of the other dozen or so operas one may be mentioned for its English background; during one of his visits to England he was shown round the Library at Buckingham Palace, and copied down some Elizabethan keyboard pieces, which he afterwards worked into the score of *Henry VIII*, an opera founded on alleged

episodes from Tudor history, and containing an astonishing ballet of Scottish dancers (*pas des Highlanders*) at Rich-
mond, accompanied by what Saint-Saëns imagined to be
Scots traditional melodies.

A scholarly interest in the music of earlier French composers was one of his most valuable contributions to the
national revival. His editions of the works of Rameau and
Gluck are still respected. He was also active as a critic,
his prose writing being distinguished by a Gallic pun-
gency. 'People have got into the bad habit of thinking
that musical sounds constitute music. It would be just
as reasonable to say that chatter is literature, or daubing
is painting.' . . . 'Fundamentally it is not Bach, or Beethoven, or Wagner that I love; it is art. I am an eclectic.'
. . . 'You young musicians, if you would accomplish aught,
insist on being French': these are a few phrases taken from
his writings. His detestation of conventions and rules of
thumb as applied to works of art is often and vigorously
expressed; in strange contrast was the unsympathetic and
even malicious attitude he adopted towards his younger
contemporaries. According to Pierre Lalo he remained
in Paris during the hottest weeks of 1902, foregoing his
usual holiday, in order to malign *Pelléas et Mélisande*.
Against d'Indy and Dukas also he bore unaccountable
grudges; yet he was capable of loyalty and generosity, as
Bizet and Fauré had good cause to remember.

His versatility was astonishing. He dabbled in many
arts and sciences; he published two volumes of verse, an
essay on the Pompeian theatre, a paper on mirages (read

before the French Astronomical Society), and some notes on the acoustics of bells. His comedy, *La crampe des écrivains*, was produced at a theatre in Algiers. During the first world war, when over eighty, he launched a pamphlet, *Germanophile*, against his country's foes. His occasional compositions ranged from a *Marche héroique* in memory of a friend who fell in the siege of Paris in 1870 to a cantata, *Le feu céleste*, written some twenty years later to celebrate the marvels of electric lighting. He was an indefatigable traveller with a passion for subtropical climates. He visited Egypt—a land that moved him to compose his fantasia *Africa* for piano and orchestra and, as already noticed, provided local colour for the Fifth Piano Concerto; the Far East; the United States; South America; and Algeria, where he settled for the last years of his long life and where he died, on the 16th December 1921.

F

FAURÉ

GABRIEL FAURÉ belongs to the second generation of those who brought about a revival of interest in non-operatic music in France during the last quarter of the nineteenth century. The first generation is represented chiefly by Franck and Saint-Saëns; but the latter was only a precocious boy of ten when Fauré was born, on the 12th May 1845. Fifteen years later, when Fauré had become a pupil at the École Niedermeyer in Paris, Saint-Saëns joined the staff as piano teacher, and his influence on Fauré was far-reaching. He made him his deputy at the Madeleine, presented him to Liszt at Weimar, and introduced him into the home of the Viardots, one of the most cultured families in Paris. In later life Fauré asserted that those of his contemporaries whose music meant most to him were Gounod, for the tenderness and delicacy of his art, and Saint-Saëns, 'parce que son écriture est une merveille de clarté et d'élégance'. Fauré inherited his preceptor's affection for the *salon* at its best, his delight in the clean line-drawing of chamber music, his pride in the control of material by intellectual discipline, something of his wide-ranging historical sympathies, and not a little of his artistic chauvinism.

After leaving the École Niedermeyer, Fauré held a series of organ appointments, first at Rennes in Brittany and later in Paris, finally becoming, at the age of fifty-one, principal organist at the Madeleine. Unlike Franck and Saint-

Saëns, he appears to have had little affection for organ-music, and left nothing of importance for the instrument. He has been compared with Schumann in that the piano enters, directly or by implication, into almost the whole of his music. The piano proved to be the ideal medium for the crystalline texture and rapidly-shifting harmonies he loved to work in. It served him equally well for the elaborate, sensuous figuration of his earlier works and for the more restrained and elliptical style of his maturity. He enriched the solo repertory of the instrument enormously. Most of his piano music is cast in the short characteristic forms first popularised by Chopin: impromptus, barcarolles, nocturnes, valse-caprices, preludes, and so on. It is easy to dismiss much of it as ephemeral salon music; and it certainly has the elegance and taste in decorative detail that are so much in keeping with the atmosphere of the nineteenth century drawing room, now fast becoming a thing of the legendary past. But these smaller pieces are always the work of an artist, and in their least profound moments call for a deft finger and an alert mind—the latter in listener as well as performer.

When the Franco-Prussian War interrupted Fauré's career some five years after it had begun he served in the ranks, and returned to Paris after the troubles of the Commune to become one of the first members of the committee of the *Société nationale de musique*. For him, as for his older colleagues, the concerts of the *Société* provided an incentive to explore the congenial territory of chamber music. Of his ten principal chamber works only one, the

String Quartet finished a few months before his death, dispenses with the piano. There are two sonatas for violin and piano, two for cello and piano, a piano trio, two piano quartets, and two piano quintets. Spread as they are over forty-eight years of the composer's life, they exhibit an interesting development of style from the first Violin Sonata (Op. 13), written in 1876, to the String Quartet, which was published posthumously. A gap of thirty-five years occurs between the earlier group of chamber works, which includes the two Piano Quartets (Op. 15 in C minor and Op. 45 in G minor) and the later group, which belongs literally as well as stylistically to the twentieth century and includes the second Violin Sonata (Op. 108 in E minor, published in 1917), the two Cello Sonatas (Op. 109 in D minor and Op. 117 in G minor, published in 1918 and 1922), the second Piano Quintet (Op. 115 in C minor, 1921), the Piano Trio (Op. 120 in D minor, 1923), and the String Quartet (Op. 121 in E minor). The first Piano Quintet (Op. 89 in D minor) occupies an intermediate position between the two groups; it was published as late as 1906, but had been in existence for fifteen years in the form of a third Piano Quartet. The first Piano Quartet, written when Fauré was in his thirties, is a fine example of his earlier manner. Its four movements have an irresistible rhythmic surge that conceals skilful organisation and economy of material. The scherzo, a type of movement that Fauré generally discards in his later works, is ingenious and witty. The harmonic language, though always spontaneously and personally used, shows but little extension of the resources of Schumann and Saint-Saëns. Keyboard figuration and general lay-out of the instrumental parts again suggest the methods of those composers. Contrast, as an example of Fauré's last-period style, the posthumous String Quartet. Here we find a spare and concise utterance that allows no redundant notes and makes no concessions to the listener. There are only three movements—Fauré generally omits the scherzo at this period—and the texture is mainly a tense polyphony that results in much dissonance and an absence of conventional cadence-points. These late chamber works are, as we shall see presently, the compositions of a deaf man, and have some of the unearthly quality we find in the later quartets of Beethoven.

A similar development of style, from early romantic luxuriance to a final and uncompromising austerity, can be traced in Fauré's solo songs. He is now recognised as one of the greatest song-writers of any country, and French music owes him a particular debt for his sensitiveness to the contemporary poetry, and especially that of Verlaine. The foundations of his sound literary taste were probably laid during his visits to the house of the Viardots, which began in 1872; he was for a time engaged to one of the daughters, Marianne Viardot. But the earliest of his songs, the twenty comprised in Opp. 1-8, had been written during or shortly after his studentship at the École Niedermeyer. They include settings of verses by Hugo, Gautier, Baudelaire, and others. Two of the most popular are *Lydia* (Op. 4, No. 2), to words by Leconte de Lisle, and

Après un rêve (Op. 7, No. 1) to words by Romain Bussine, one of the founders of the *Société nationale*. More than twenty years later he turned with fresh enthusiasm to song-writing, and it was now that he found himself attracted by the poems of Verlaine. *Clair de lune* (Op. 46, No. 2) is one of the first and best known of his Verlaine settings. Another important group (Op. 58) was written in Venice, where, in 1890, Fauré had been enabled to take a holiday at the expense of that notable benefactor of musicians, the Princesse de Polignac. The set contains *Mandoline*, with its delicate accompaniment and its voice-part suggesting in its subtle rhythm and cadences and eloquent melismata the influence of the plainsong that made up so important a part of Fauré's background. The piano arpeggios and elusive harmonic progressions of *En sourdine* make this song closely akin to the instrumental sonatas. In the year following the Venice songs Fauré set a group of nine poems by Verlaine under the title of *La bonne chanson* (Op. 61), which represents perhaps the culmination, though certainly not the conclusion, of Fauré's career as a song-writer. It is a true song-cycle, responsive to all the changing moods of the poet-lover, and rounding off the whole story with a song, *L'hiver a cessé*, that brings to fulfilment a number of musical ideas from earlier songs in the cycle. Not least among the excellences of *La bonne chanson* is the maturity of the harmonic idiom at which Fauré had by this time arrived; major and minor, the older modes, diatonic and chromatic chords, are fused into a new system that is unfettered by the classical tonic-dominant

relationship and yet has a convincing logic of its own. Of
the songs written after the turn of the century those written to texts by the Belgian poet Charles van Lerberghe
must be mentioned: *La chanson d'Ève* (Op. 95) and *Le
jardin clos* (Op. 106). These are parallel to the later chamber music, and possess the same characteristics; diatonic,
rather than chromatic, melodic progressions are now the
rule; the harmony tends to be elliptical and altogether
unexpected; the texture is spare and above all economical.
Fauré's last group of songs, *L'horizon chimérique* (Op. 118),
to words by Jean de la Ville de Mirmont, a young poet
who was killed in the first world war, was written in 1922.

Colour, in the instrumental sense, plays only a minor
part in Fauré's music; if the language of the visual arts is
to be used, it would be more fitting to speak of shades or
tones. Neither the organ, as we have seen, nor the orchestra seems to have held much interest for him. Even the
two of his works that have passed into the orchestral repertory—the Suite *Masques et Bergamasques* and the *Pavane*
(with optional chorus) have won favour more because of
their charm of melody and gracefulness of form, and because of a pleasingly archaic flavour, than through any
distinction of scoring. Orchestration as such seems to have
interested him so little that he was sometimes content to
leave it to another hand. It is therefore difficult to deter-
mine how much of the scoring of his stage music is his
own, though excerpts from the music to Haraucourt's *Shylock* and Maeterlinck's *Pelléas et Mélisande* are occasionally included in orchestral programmes. His one attempt

at a symphony, made at the age of forty, he suppressed. There is, however, one work that demonstrates his ability to use orchestral resources, when he chose, with discretion and practical competence.

In 1877 Fauré had become second organist and choirmaster at the Madeleine; not until 1896 did he succeed Dubois as principal organist. In 1885 the composer's father died, and three years later Fauré gave at the Madeleine the first performance of a *Requiem* written in memory of his father. The work is liturgically conceived, and is of the most poignant simplicity. The usual full orchestra is employed, with harp and organ, but without oboes; violas and cellos are divided throughout, imparting a sombre colouring to the score; the violins are silent during the whole of the first two movements until the Sanctus is reached. Wind instruments are even more sparingly used. A spirit of tenderness broods over the whole work; the omission of the *Dies Irae* from the text, and the choice of the antiphon *In Paradisum* for the concluding movement, allows the composer to avoid depicting the terrors of the Last Judgment and to dwell upon the assurance of salvation and peace.

Contemporary with the *Requiem* is the first of Fauré's attempts to write for the stage. He began, in 1888, with choruses and interludes for *Caligula*, a tragedy by Alexandre Dumas. In the following year he composed for *Shylock*, an adaptation from *The Merchant of Venice*, a series of delicate pieces that can still be heard fairly often in the form of an orchestral suite. The next commission of this kind came from the Prince of Wales Theatre, London, in 1898, when Maeterlinck's *Pelléas et Mélisande* was produced in English. Fauré came himself to London to conduct the music, which included a song and several interludes. Most of this music too has survived in the orchestral repertory; the scoring, however, is not Fauré's own but was carried out by his pupil and biographer, Charles Koechlin. On a more elaborate scale was Fauré's contribution to *Prométhée*, a drama on classical lines staged in August 1900 in the reconstructed open-air amphitheatre belonging to the town of Béziers. Earlier productions of the same kind had been supplied with music by Saint-Saëns, who was also present on this occasion and conducted (in a straw hat) the prelude to Fauré's music. In spite of the unusual conditions of performance, which included an orchestra made up of amateur strings, the local military band, and a bevy of harps, Fauré seems to have enjoyed the opportunities offered him by such situations as the funeral procession of Pandora and the chorus of the Oceanides. *Prométhée* was performed three times on successive days, the Béziers festival concluding with a concert of works by Saint-Saëns. Fauré wrote only one full-length opera: *Pénélope*, produced for the first time at Monte Carlo in 1913, when the composer was sixty-eight. Avoiding on the one hand the set 'numbers' of pre-Wagnerian opera, and on the other the intricate developments of Wagner's own plots and scores, Fauré aims at a classical restraint, and ends his work in a mood of tranquillity that recalls the close of the *Requiem*.

Besides his creative work as a composer Fauré achieved a high reputation and wide influence as teacher and critic. In 1892 he was made Inspector of State Conservatoires throughout France. In 1896, the year in which he became organist at the Madeleine, he was appointed professor of composition at the Paris Conservatoire in succession to Massenet. In 1905 he followed Dubois as Director of the Conservatoire. His rule lasted fifteen years until, at the age of seventy-five, increasing deafness obliged him to resign. He reformed the curriculum of the Conservatoire, striving to give the students what he himself had received from the progressive Niedermeyer institution—a broad cultural horizon and a sympathetic understanding of the best music of all periods. As a critic Fauré was connected chiefly with the journal *Figaro*. He wrote thoughtfully on contemporary composers, including Grieg and Puccini, as well as on the accepted classics.

Fauré died in Paris on the 4th November 1924. He had passed the last four years of his life in retirement, but not in idleness; as we have seen, the Second Piano Quintet, the second Cello Sonata, the song cycle *L'horizon chimérique*, and the String Quartet were among the remarkable products of his vigorous intellect and indomitable will, and crowned his achievement as an exemplar of those qualities he himself considered to belong to the best of French art: 'clarity of thought, gravity and purity of form, sincerity, and scorn for crude effect.'

DEBUSSY

To the English music-lover brought up chiefly on the Italian, Austrian, and German classics it is not always easy to trace a clear pattern in the course of French musical history. What thread of connection, if any, exists between composers as widely different in style and scope as Rameau, Berlioz, Gounod, d'Indy, and Ravel? How far, if at all, did a Gallic spirit influence immigrant composers from neighbouring lands, such as Gluck, Cherubini, Chopin, and Franck? Was the career of Debussy, to come to the subject of this chapter, in any important sense a fulfilment of French artistic ideals, or must it be regarded as the outcome of an innovating temperament in revolt against both present and past? It may be worth while to try to place this highly original composer in some kind of historical perspective.

Achille-Claude Debussy was born on the 22nd August 1862 in Saint-Germain-en-Laye, near Paris, but spent several years of his childhood at Cannes, where he had piano lessons from a Mme Mauté de Fleurville, who had been a pupil of Chopin, and was further distinguished as being the mother-in-law of Verlaine. At the age of eleven he was admitted to the Paris Conservatoire, where he soon gained a reputation as a somewhat tiresome student. He was unimpressed by the 'seraphic' idealism of Franck, admired composers of lighter calibre like Offenbach, Delibes, Massenet, and Sullivan (he heard *Pinafore* while on a visit to London in 1878), and often scandalised the conservative Durand, of whose harmony class he was a refractory member, with apparently wilful and illogical dissonances.

Towards the close of his student days Debussy lived for some weeks as pianist and teacher in the household of Madame von Meck, the patroness of Tchaikovsky, and about a year later, in 1881, followed the family to Russia. It is possible that he may have obtained there at first hand a slight knowledge of the work of the Russian nationalist composers that was soon to exert an important influence on the French music of his own generation. Another friendship that meant much to him was that of Mme Vasnier, a cultured and beautiful woman who invited Debussy to her home, sang to his accompaniment, and introduced him to the poets Verlaine and Mallarmé. It was at this time that he wrote his earliest settings of Verlaine's *Fêtes galantes*.

In 1884 Debussy won the *premier Grand-Prix de Rome* with a cantata, *L'enfant prodigue*. During the next two years he lived in Italy at the Villa Medici, composing without much enthusiasm the *envois*, or works prescribed by the terms of his scholarship, studying the music of various periods from Palestrina to Wagner, and meeting several eminent figures in the musical world of the time, including Verdi and Liszt. But he found the artistic associations of Italy less inspiring than the vitality of his beloved Paris; so much so that he left Rome without completing the stipulated three years' residence, returned to France, and for the next few years immersed himself in the complex literary and artistic movements that were rife in the capital. The music of Wagner, then at the height of his vogue in France, the poetry of the Symbolists, the painting of Degas and Fantin-Latour, glimpses of exciting rhythmic and harmonic idioms of the Russian school, the novelty of the exotic music of Eastern Europe, Africa, and Asia revealed at the Paris Universal Exhibition of 1889, all made their impressions on Debussy at a most receptive period of his life. A new world of sound seemed to be opening around him, made up of elements as diverse as the multi-coloured orchestra of *Tristan*, the primitive rhythms and strange scales of Indonesian music, and the use of verbal symbols in poetry to produce a simultaneous effect on the ear and the mind. It has always been part of the artistic genius of the French people to fuse and ac-climatise such strangely assorted elements, and Debussy shared that genius to the full. In his eagerness to learn from his contemporaries, however different in tempera-ment they might be, he sought out Brahms in Vienna in 1887 and during the next two years visited Bayreuth to hear *Tristan*, *Meistersinger*, and *Parsifal*.

So far, Debussy had produced little of his own that has more than an historical interest: the orchestral suite *Printemps*, and the pre-Raphaelite cantata *La demoiselle élue*—two of his *envois de Rome*, the popular *Petite suite*, the *Arabesques*, and the *Suite bergamasque* for piano, and some settings of poems by Verlaine and Baudelaire are among the exceptions. At the age of thirty he was still forming his style, which in spite of many signs of an in-

dividual outlook and technique retained at this period a
great deal of the rather insipid grace and prettiness we associate chiefly with Gounod and Massenet. On the other
hand, he had maintained a resistance to the prevalent
Wagner fever and when he achieved an operatic work it
proved to be radically different from anything that had
come out of Bayreuth. But this is to anticipate; although
he came across Maeterlinck's *Pelléas et Mélisande* in 1892
the completion and production of the score were to take
another ten years.

The real Debussy first emerged on the 22nd December
1894, when the orchestral *Prélude à l'Après-midi d'un faune*
was performed at a concert of the *Société nationale*. This
piece, inspired by a poem of Mallarmé, was originally
intended as the first part of a triptych. It remains one of
the freshest pieces in the standard orchestral repertory,
a wonderfully successful experiment in using effects of
sound in a way that no composer had hitherto attempted,
although there are foreshadowings of it in Liszt, Borodin,
Grieg, and others. The term 'impressionism' used to describe it covers an original treatment of melody, harmony,
construction, and instrumentation which can be fairly aptly
illustrated from the first four bars of *L'Après-midi*; the
opening phrases, in the lowest register of the flute, seem
deliberately contrived to deceive the listener as to the exact moment when the music begins, and the chord touched
in by woodwind and horn has its outlines softened by the
glissando of the harp. The technique has been compared
to the pointillist methods of the impressionist painters.

A little earlier than *L'Après-midi* Debussy had produced
the first of his chamber works, the String Quartet with
its Spanish-sounding scherzo and its cyclic use of the
same theme in all its four movements. It was first performed, with the cantata *La demoiselle élue*, at a concert
of the *Société nationale* in 1893. Another work that occupied much of Debussy's energies during the nineties was
the *Nocturnes*, now known as an orchestral suite of three
pieces but originally conceived for violin and orchestra. It
is thought that Debussy may have taken the title *Nocturnes*
from the impressionistic paintings of Whistler. The first
of the three pieces, *Nuages*, is an attempt to create in
musical sound a counterpart to the painter's response to
shifting lights and shadows. The second pieces, *Fêtes*, is
memorable for its use of the brass in a vivid march-like
rhythm, as typically French as the brass entries of Elgar's
Cockaigne are British. The suite is completed by *Sirènes*,
where the wordless harmonies of a women's choir add a
new colour to the orchestral palette. Debussy perhaps
never surpassed his own mastery of orchestral effect as
shown in the *Nocturnes*, though his three symphonic sketches known as *La Mer*, completed (at Eastbourne, of all
places) in 1905, are even grander in imaginative design
and richer in decorative beauty. While they record, no
doubt, impressions derived from Debussy's early love of
the sea and bear, like so many of his later piano pieces,
descriptive titles: *De l'aube à midi sur la mer*, *Jeux de
vagues*, and *Dialogue du vent et de la mer*, there is nothing
of the understatement and formlessness so often, and so

wrongly, associated with impressionism both in painting and in music. Erik Satie's famous *mot* about enjoying *De l'aube à midi* and especially 'the bit at a quarter to eleven', implied a whimsical recognition of the work as pure music. After completing *La Mer* Debussy reverted to small-scale composition, chiefly for the piano; only in the *Images* (*Iberia*, 1908; *Rondes de printemps*, 1909; *Gigues*, 1912), did he again attempt larger works for the orchestra.

Debussy's personal behaviour, always inscrutable and unaccountable, had by now become more mysterious than ever. After living for about ten years with a woman who was always referred to as 'Gaby' he suddenly, on the 19th November 1899, married Rosalie Texier, a dressmaker who had for some time been a member of the Bohemian circle in which Debussy lived. Less than five years later Debussy shocked and estranged most of his friends by leaving 'Lily' abruptly and eventually marrying Emma Bardac, an excellent singer; this seems to have been a happy marriage, and the child of it was the 'Chou-chou' for whom the composer wrote his piano suite, *The Children's Corner*.

After many revisions extending over ten years the opera *Pelléas et Mélisande* was produced, with the Scottish singer Mary Garden as Mélisande, in 1902. Romain Rolland regarded this event as marking the full emancipation of French music. Apart from the shadowy beauty of its general musical style, *Pelléas* shows Debussy as the most sensitive of all French musicians who have attempted to set their own language. In achieving a variety of recitative that faithfully reproduces the nuances of speech, while creating at the same time a musically satisfying, though slender, texture, he performed something of the same service to the French language as Mussorgsky did to the Russian. In some sense, too, *Pelléas* is a return to the aims and principles of the early seventeenth century school of Italian composers, with their monodic recitative supported by accompaniments that are unobtrusive but colourful. Debussy employs an orchestra of Wagnerian dimensions, used not to create an overwhelming mass of sound or to develop, on an equality with the voices, the musical material of the drama as with Wagner, but to provide a background of subdued but ever-changing colours to a handful of characters. There are no 'concerted' passages, no chorus, no ballet. There was no wonder that Paris received the opera for the most part with coldness or open hostility. *Pelléas et Mélisande* is now accepted as a classic of the operatic repertory, but it is also a *tour de force* that cannot be repeated or imitated.

Few opportunities occur for an English audience to hear *Pelléas*, but it is far otherwise with the composer's piano works, many of which are now almost as familiar to the amateur pianist as those of Chopin. Somewhat confusingly, the title *Images* was given not only to the orchestral pieces already mentioned but also to two sets of piano pieces written about the same time. The title of one of them, *Hommage à Rameau*, is an allusion to the composer's interest in French keyboard music of the seventeenth century, and thus forms a sequel to the early *Suite berga-*

G

masque. One piece is called simply *Mouvement*; the others are picturesque—*Reflets dans l'eau, Cloches à travers les feuilles*—again the merging of light and sound into a single sense-impression—and two inspired by oriental art: *Poissons d'or* and *Et la lune descend sur le temple qui fut.* *Estampes*, written two years before the piano *Images*, suggest in their titles Debussy's interest in oriental scales and instrumentation (*Pagodes*), Spanish dance-rhythms (*Soirée dans Grenade*), and the music of children (*Jardins sous la pluie*, where two nursery tunes are quoted). The later sets of piano pieces are miniatures, some with touches of satire, others full of poetic feeling. *The Children's Corner* (1908) and the twenty-four *Préludes* (two books, 1910 and 1913)—some of the latter only a page or two in length —present various aspects of impressionism in forms that have made them among the most accessible of Debussy's works.

By the time he was fifty Debussy was in the grip of a painful disease. Yet he had still much to do, and battled bravely on. He travelled a great deal, for he was in demand as a conductor of his own works. Oddly enough, Spain was not among the countries he visited, despite his wonderfully successful evocations of the Spanish spirit in several of the piano pieces. To this period belong his experiments in mime and ballet, including the music for d'Annunzio's play *Le martyre de saint Sébastien*, the tennis ballet *Jeux* written for Diaghilev in 1912, and the children's fantasy *La boîte à joujoux*. The outbreak of war in 1914 made a pause in his creative activity, but after a year or two he came forward as a champion of Gallic art, subscribing himself in his publications *Musicien français*. His desire to compose also returned, and in addition to a number of occasional pieces inspired by patriotism he embarked upon a series of works remarkable for the complete absence of literary or picturqesue suggestion in their titles or content: the twelve *Études* for piano, and the three sonatas: one for cello and piano, one for flute, viola, and harp, and one for violin and piano, his last completed work. Three more sonatas had been projected. The style of these last works indicates that Debussy was entering on a new period of development, and one cannot help wondering whether Debussy would, like Fauré, have produced an important body of chamber music if he had been allowed another ten years of life. But this was not to be; on the 25th March 1918, when the German long-range guns were trained on Paris, Debussy died at the age of fifty-six.

He bequeathed to his art a new harmonic and rhythmic freedom. He had opened fresh paths by his exploitation of the medieval modes and the pentatonic scale, the freer employment of pedal notes, the bold use of diatonic discords, the development of block harmony, the treatment of acoustical effects as material for serious music. All these, and many more, are among the accepted resources of modern composition and are taken for granted even by the popular hack 'arranger' and by the writers of the feeblest type of song and piano piece. Not even Wagner has had a more extensive influence on the language of music.

ELGAR

To a foreign observer, contemplating the chalky cliffs of the land without music, the appearance of Elgar in the first rank of English music during the last years of the nineteenth century must have seemed in consonance with the incalculable course of our history and the paradoxical nature of our political and social institutions. Here, in a country whose musical policy seemed determined mainly by academically-trained holders of university, college, and cathedral posts, a musician had emerged self-taught and had, moreover, asserted his claims as a composer by vocation. A Roman Catholic, he had stormed the Protestant citadel of oratorio. In the midst of a nation of organists he had somehow or other learnt spells to unleash the magic powers of the modern orchestra. In appearance and habits he was the middle class cultured Englishman to the point of caricature; and yet he was an eccentric in the literal sense—a man and a musician who appeared somehow to have strayed out of his orbit.

But to those who knew their England it might not have seemed altogether strange that Elgar should have been produced by an environment that had nurtured other artists before him. When he was born, on the 2nd June 1857, at Broadheath in Worcestershire, the English countryside was probably as beautiful as it had ever been, and certainly more beautiful than it can ever be again. The social and intellectual life of a town like Worcester and of its en-

virons was varied, virile, and full of character. The cathedral, playing its part in the Three Choirs Festival, and
other churches of various denominations were recognised
and beloved centres of musical activity. So, in its own
way, was the music shop in Worcester where W. H. Elgar
sold copies of *Messiah*, the waltzes of Strauss and Lanner,
and occasionally the full score of a Beethoven symphony,
and from which he set out on horseback to tune the pianos
of the county families, or on foot to play the organ at St.
George's Roman Catholic church, or to take a violin or
viola part in a local orchestra or chamber music circle.

Against a background like this the young Elgar learnt
his craft, doing apprentice's and later journeyman's work
at the organ console and violin desk, accompanying and
conducting the Worcester Glee Club, teaching in the young
ladies' schools in which the district abounded, picking up
the technique of bassoon or trombone as occasion required
the filling of a gap in a family wind quintet or the county
mental asylum orchestra. His was an all-round intellect
that fed not only on the scores and text-books of his
father's stock but also on the literature of more than one
language. A few months spent in a lawyer's office were
scarcely an interruption in his progress towards the status
of a versatile and respected young local musician. Stages
of the journey were a term of experience in Stockley's
orchestra in Birmingham, a brief course of violin lessons
in London under Pollitzer, a visit to Leipzig, and performances in Birmingham and Worcester of some early works
like the *Sérénade mauresque* and *Sevillana*. These were

trifles, but their charm and certainty of effect brought him wider opportunities. In the autumn of 1890, rather more than a year after his marriage to Caroline Alice Roberts, he conducted at the Worcester Festival his concert overture *Froissart* (Op. 19). This, his first large-scale work to be published, and the cantata, *The Black Knight* (Op. 25), stood out among a quantity of part-songs and drawing room pieces. A less pretentious work, the *Serenade* for Strings (Op. 20), has a quiet sincerity and charm that ensure its popularity through changes of fashion; it is rich in those spacious diatonic themes that look so obvious on paper but when heard make an indescribable impression of originality. Less in worth, but historically important because it was one of the first of his works to be heard at the Promenade Concerts, was the secular cantata, *Scenes from the Bavarian Highlands* (Op. 27). This was in the heyday of the English choral society and the provincial choir festival, with their insatiable demands for new material from composers of every degree of eminence. No English musician, however independent his attitude and however strong his desire to write instrumental works, could afford to neglect the field of the cantata and the oratorio. *The Black Knight* was succeeded by *Lux Christi*, *King Olaf*, and *The Banner of St. George*, the last of which like the *Imperial March* strikes boldly though sincerely the note of patriotism that the Diamond Jubilee of 1897 called forth and marked the beginning of Elgar's honoured career as the musical laureate of British imperialism in its final and most resplendent phase. *Caractacus*, again on a national theme and dedicated to the Queen, completed the recognition of Elgar as a composer of much more than provincial repute.

But in proportion as his works came to be heard more often in London and other great cities Elgar found greater pleasure and satisfaction in the countryside, with its Worcestershire 'characters', that had been his background all his life. He was an artist in friendship, and the *Variations on an Original Theme* (Op. 36) show him returning, at the height of his success in the music of pageantry, to the richer variety of his own personality and those of his friends. Much time has been wasted on speculation about the 'enigma' said to be propounded in the theme; the real marvel lies in the unity of the *Variations* as a work of art. The great 'Nimrod' Variation has been styled one of the finest orchestral adagios since Beethoven.

The moment was at hand when Elgar's stature was to find recognition abroad. During a visit to England, Hans Richter had come across the Variations and had insisted on carrying a copy of the score home with him. And so it was in Germany, at the Düsseldorf Festival of 1901, that *The Dream of Gerontius* received its first satisfactory performance—an earlier one in England had been a lamentable travesty. Elgar had meditated on Newman's poem for eleven years before he felt his style was mature enough to allow him to set it fittingly. The final result was oratorio raised to a new power. The music owes much to Wagner's *Parsifal*, not a little to Dvořák, who at one time had thought of setting *Gerontius* himself, and something to Franck; yet Elgar's personality transcends all extraneous influences, and in certain passages, like the opening phrases of the violas and woodwind, or the heavenly three-part string writing of the Introduction to the second part of the oratorio, achieves its most concentrated expression.

The next important group of Elgar's works shows a swing back from the mystical to the imperialist style; the overture *Cockaigne* (Op. 40) and the *Pomp and Circumstance* Marches (Op. 39) and the *Coronation Ode* (Op. 44), evoking the gay, self-assured spirit of Edwardian London, already have a period flavour that is not without a touch of pathos. These things, it must be repeated, meant much to the composer and unlike some of his more hypersensitive contemporaries he was not ashamed of his gift for writing what are, in the best sense, vulgar tunes. He could shake them gladly and generously from his capacious sleeve and turn with equal enthusiasm to the setting for male voices of five austere poems from the Greek Anthology (Op. 45).

The year 1903, with the interesting but still comparatively unknown oratorio *The Apostles* (Op. 49), and the planning of an Elgar festival to be held in March of the following year, marks his full rise to fame. The festival included performances in Covent Garden Theatre of *The Dream of Gerontius*, the *Enigma Variations*, *Cockaigne*, and the elaborate and lengthy overture *In the South* (Op. 50) inspired by a holiday in Italy. A few months later came further honours: a knighthood, and an appointment to the newly-founded Peyton Chair of Music in Birmingham

University. The delivery of academic lectures proved, however, less congenial to Elgar than conducting the London Symphony Orchestra in a series of tours that began in 1905 and gave him still firmer command of orchestral resources. His gifts of clear and brilliant scoring, recognised even by those who were most strongly antipathetic towards his music as a whole, matured during these years, and came to full ripeness in a series of massive orchestral compositions. The *Introduction and Allegro* for String Quartet and Orchestra is an interesting, and comparatively early, example of the modern tendency to revive the schemes of the old *concerto grosso* and to find in fugal texture a satisfying way to rhythmic freedom; it is, moreover, a masterly exploitation of the sonorities of stringed instruments, of whose capabilities Elgar himself declared he had learnt most by studying the scores of Handel and 'listening to his second violins'. Five years later, in 1910, Fritz Kreisler gave the first public performance of the Violin Concerto, where the claims of the modern solo concerto are reasserted in writing of overwhelming brilliance; the first utterance of the solo instrument, a quiet phrase in a low register, is in itself a stroke of genius.

On either side of the Violin Concerto stand the two Symphonies (Op. 55 and Op. 63). The First Symphony, in A flat, was in Elgar's mind for many years until, having passed the age of fifty, he decided upon its form and scoring. The traditional four movements are interrelated by certain transferences and transformations of theme, a procedure that had become almost a convention at the period

H

with the symphonies of Franck, Dvořák, and Tchaikovsky; Elgar carries it out with conviction, ending the finale
with the same resolute diatonic phrase with which the
Symphony opens. The Second Symphony, in E flat, was
begun a year or so after the completion of the First, and
was originally intended to be dedicated to King Edward
VII. After the King's death in 1910 Elgar wrote the slow
movement as an elegiac tribute; it has the character of a
funeral march, and to-day affects the hearer as a palinode,
not on any individual, but on the spacious period that
ended with the catastrophe of 1914. The Cello Concerto
(Op. 85), like the little group of chamber works—a Sonata
for Violin and Piano (Op. 82), a String Quartet (Op. 83),
and a Piano Quintet (Op. 84)—appeared towards the end,
or just after the end, of the first World War. For some
admirers of Elgar's music his finest orchestral work is the
Symphonic Study *Falstaff* (Op. 68). Here the composer
challenges his great German contemporary and friend,
Richard Strauss; *Falstaff* undoubtedly owes something to
Till Eulenspiegel, especially in the treatment of episodes,
but in material and style it is completely and unmistak-
ably Elgarian. The trite adjective 'mellow' is the one that
seems best to describe the humour, the tenderness, and
above all the ripe intelligence of this entrancing work.

The end of the first World War marks the end, or almost the end, of Elgar's creative life. He never recovered
completely from the shock of Lady Elgar's death in 1920.
He worked fitfully upon a third part of the trilogy of
which *The Apostles* and *The Kingdom* were intended as

the first two sections; the whole trilogy was to have been knit together by the use of certain themes. In the completed oratorios much stress is laid on the delineation of human personality as well as on the mystical idea of the growth of a Church, and the dramatic element also is strong in such episodes as the remorse of Judas, in *The Apostles*, which is portrayed against the background of an ancient Hebrew psalm chanted within the Temple. It seemed possible during these last years that Elgar would find another outlet for his sense of dramatic effect; an opera, *The Spanish Lady*, based on Ben Jonson's *The Devil is an Ass*, was planned with Sir Barry Jackson, and Elgar made many sketches for the music. Another major work undertaken soon after the celebrations attendant on Elgar's seventy-fifth birthday was a Third Symphony, commissioned by the B.B.C. He was in the midst of this task when he died, in his own house at Worcester, on the 23rd February 1934.

MAHLER

GUSTAV MAHLER was born of Jewish parents at Kališt in Bohemia on the 7th July 1860. His childhood was blighted by poverty, ill-health, both physical and mental, and brutal treatment. A scoundrelly father and an all too patient mother, sickness of body and mind throughout the whole of a large family, made up a dark background relieved only by flashes of the supernormal imagination of a gifted, highly-strung child. It is not hard to believe that these early experiences account for Mahler's lifelong preoccupation with the joys and griefs of children and for an element of the childlike that is constantly coming to the surface of his complicated, introspective nature.

At the age of fifteen Mahler entered the Vienna Conservatory, and on the completion of a three years' course there was appointed Kapellmeister in the town of Hall. From here he graduated, by way of similar posts in Laibach and Olmütz, to some of the most important musical centres of Europe: first Vienna, where he acted for a few months as chorus-master at the Carltheater; then to Cassel; in 1885 to Prague; the following year to Leipzig, as second-in-command to Nikisch; in 1888 to Budapest; in 1891 to Hamburg, where he remained for six years, and where he first met a young chorus-master who, under the name of Bruno Walter, was subsequently to become Mahler's most enthusiastic and influential apostle; and finally, at the age of thirty-seven, to the Hofoper in Vienna.

This responsible appointment had been given him mainly on the recommendation of Brahms, who had been strongly impressed by the excellence of Mahler's work at Budapest. During the ten years of his rule over the Vienna opera he strove with ruthless determination to satisfy his high artistic ideals. In 1902 he married Alma Schindler, a woman of considerable artistic sensibility who had received training both as a sculptor and as a musician. Their first child died in 1907, and it was this bereavement, and his own indifferent health, that induced Mahler to resign his post in Vienna and accept one with somewhat lighter duties in America. He seems to have felt also that he had given of his best to the Vienna opera and could only repeat his successes there. In 1907 and 1908 he conducted the New York Philharmonic Orchestra. In 1910 he visited America for the third time, was taken seriously ill with heart disease, and shortly after his return to Austria died on the 18th May 1911.

Mahler's first important composition was the romantic ballad *Das klagende Lied*. For this he wrote the verses— a morbid treatment of a macabre theme—beginning both them and the music in 1878 and finishing the work about two years later. It was planned first as an opera, but was soon turned into a concert work for soloists, chorus, and orchestra. Twenty years after, in 1898 and 1900, it was published in revised form. In 1883 Mahler visited Bayreuth to hear *Parsifal*; and nothing shows more plainly the original turn of his musical thought than that he produced soon afterwards, not a sedulous imitation of Wagner in music-drama, or even in symphony or symphonic poem, but the song-cycle *Lieder eines fahrenden Gesellen*, wherein the resources of the modern orchestra are used with a restraint comparable to that of Verdi in his last operas, while the voice-part, following a text of Mahler's own, is patterned not on Wagner's 'endless melody' but on the ingenuous phrases of German folk-song.

The melodies of two of the *Lieder* reappear in the third and fourth movements of the First Symphony, in D, which was first performed in Budapest in 1889. In the full range and transparency of its colouring this work makes a useful introduction to the composer's symphonic style. Some of its elements are inherited from the early nineteenth century: the woodland bird and hunting calls of the first movement, the funeral procession of the third (suggested by a picture called 'The Huntsman's Funeral', and based musically on the children's round 'frère Jacques'), the tearing discord leading from the third to the fourth move-ment—recalling the corresponding moment in Beethoven's Ninth Symphony—and above all the march-rhythms that pervade Viennese music from Mozart onwards. The com-position of the Second Symphony, in C minor, overlaps that of the First, but the complete work was not heard in public until 1895, when Mahler had it performed at his own expense—to ensure adequate rehearsal of the huge forces involved—in Berlin. The score is that of an idealist, demanding as it does quadruple woodwind, twenty-five brass instruments, two harps, organ, three timpanists, five percussion players, organ, and strings 'all in the greatest

possible strength'. Solo singers and a chorus are also required. But it is also that of a practical idealist, for the
huge orchestra is used not as a means of making noise but
as a vast colour-palette, and conductor and players are
given the most explicit directions on every conceivable
point of execution and interpretation: *Schalltrichter in die
Höhe* (to woodwind players, telling them to raise the bells
of their instruments); *Von hier allmählich und unmerklich
zu Tempo I. zurückkehren* (a gradual resumption of Tempo
I); and a stern warning to horn players who have been
playing 'off-stage' (*In der Ferne*) not to disturb the singing
of the unaccompanied chorus while resuming their places
in the orchestra.

In this Symphony we meet with a number of features of
construction and style that will reappear in later works.
At the end of the first movement, which was originally
called 'Funeral Pomp', Mahler directs that a pause of at
least five minutes shall elapse before the beginning of the
next movement. The second movement has the Ländler
rhythm that appealed so much to the Viennese in Mahler;
he was to use it again in the Ninth Symphony. In the
remaining movements come the first of those associations
between symphony and song that constitute an essential
part of Mahler's conception of the medium. The third
movement is based on his setting of 'St. Anthony preach-
ing to the fishes', one of the twelve songs from *Des Knaben
Wunderhorn* that he wrote in 1892-5. In the fourth movement a solo voice is introduced, an alto, with a setting of
a mystical poem from the same collection, and in the fifth

the chorus enters with a chorale based on a poem by Klop-
stock, 'Resurrection'.

As the collection entitled *Des Knaben Wunderhorn* (The
boy's magic horn) plays so important a part in Mahler's
work a word must be said about it here. It is a large collection of folk-poetry, including nursery rhymes, made by
two writers, Arnim and Brentano, and first published in
1805. Although the *Wunderhorn* had considerable influence on the Romantic poets, few musical settings of the
poems themselves appear to have been made until Mahler
came across them for the first time in 1888. He found in
them an echo of his own childish fantasies, and drew upon
them repeatedly for solo songs and for vocal passages in
the Symphonies. Not only the Second, as we have seen,
but also the Third and Fourth Symphonies contain movements based on *Wunderhorn* texts.

The Third Symphony, in D minor, often called the
'Nature' Symphony, was begun in 1895 during a holiday
at Steinbach in the Salzkammergut, beside the Altensee,
and waited six years for its first public performance at
Krefeld. In its first draft this work comprised seven movements, each based on some aspect of Nature; later Mahler
considered developing this scheme on philosophical lines,
leading from the love of inanimate Nature up to the love
of God. As completed in 1896, the Symphony contains
six movements: the first an echo of an Austrian military
march, and suggesting in its opening horn theme a well-
known students' song, the second in the style of a minuet,
the third somewhat in the manner of a Schubertian rondo

with posthorn episodes and based on one of Mahler's *Wunderhorn* songs, the fourth a setting for solo alto of a text from Nietzsche, the fifth a setting for female voices of another *Wunderhorn* text, and the sixth a solemn instrumental postlude. The work foreshadows the Eighth Symphony in being divided into two sections, the first comprising the huge first movement, the second the remaining five movements, and its original programmatic conception is apparent in the diffuse and rhapsodic style. The most picturesque movement is the fifth; violins are omitted from the score, but there is a large force of woodwind, and also harps, glockenspiel, bells, and a choir of boys to supply additional bell effects through vocalisation.

In the Fourth Symphony, in G, there is the same apparent incongruity of a childlike fancy at play against a tragic background. The first movement, with its naïvely realistic sleigh-bells, is said to be an impression of the pleasant hilly countryside around Vienna as viewed during a carriage-ride. Lovely soaring, singing melodies well up at every moment. The second movement is one that Berlioz would have appreciated, and perhaps Saint-Saëns too; for it originated in the old pictorial theme of the Dance of Death, and is dominated by the strident sounds of a solo violin. Mahler's subjective romanticism and love of song culminate in the fourth movement, where a solo soprano sings a setting of 'The Heavenly Joy' from the *Wunderhorn*[1] — a picturesque, mock-materialistic set

---

[1] In the *Wundernhorn* these verses (described as a Bavarian folk-song) are entitled *Der Himmel hangt voll Geigen*.

of verses somewhat suggestive of the fabled land of Cockaigne.

The motive of idealised childhood recurs in the *Kindertotenlieder* (Songs on the Death of Children), the words of which are by Rückert and allude to the loss of his own children. Mahler's own bereavement came later; he was in the full enjoyment of a happy family life when he wrote these poignant settings.

In the Fifth, Sixth, and Seventh Symphonies, composed between 1901 and 1905, Mahler restricts himself to purely instrumental forces on a vast scale; the Sixth, for example, makes use of quadruple woodwind, eight horns, four trumpets, and an immense battery of percussion instruments. The Fifth Symphony contains a popular *Adagietto*, but the most interesting of the group is perhaps the Seventh Symphony, first performed at Prague in 1908. Its five movements, two of them called *Nachtmusik*, suggest that Mahler was at this stage being influenced in his symphonic writing by the eighteenth century suite; a similar tendency, indeed, can be observed as early as the Third Symphony. The sketches of the incomplete Tenth also indicate that there were to have been five movements. In the opening of the first *Nachtmusik* one is struck by the 'linear' texture of the counterpoint woven by woodwind and horns; the other *Nachtmusik* has a very characteristic colouring of plucked strings, with harp, mandoline, and guitar figuring in the score. The Scherzo (marked *schattenhaft*—'shadowy') resembles the corresponding movement in the Sixth Symphony, in that both have a remarkable part for the timpani. The military march element is also strong in the first movements of both Symphonies.

The Eighth Symphony, first performed in Munich in 1910, again introduces the human voice. This is the 'Symphony of the Thousand', which the composer referred to as a 'Barnum and Bailey show', with an assemblage of double mixed voice chorus, children's chorus, seven solo voices, organ, and large orchestra. This gigantic work is divided into two parts: the first, an elaborate choral setting of *Veni Creator Spiritus*; the second, a setting for solo voices, choirs, and orchestra of the closing scene from Goethe's *Faust*, whose mystical quality the composer strives to enhance by every device of texture, dynamics, and colouring his imagination and science can call upon. A hearing of this work, and an examination of the score, are apt to raise the same doubts that occur in connection with its ancestor, Beethoven's Ninth Symphony: namely, whether the composer's vision has not carried him beyond what can be expressed in sound. But this is the dilemma that faces all who try to communicate a mystical experience in any medium.

'The Song of the Earth' (*Das Lied von der Erde*) occupies a special position among Mahler's works. It is generally considered to be not only his most characteristic but also his most satisfying composition. Here his unfailing fount of melody, poured out in song, his mastery of the orchestra, and his poetic sweetness are uninhibited by the conflicts and exertions of symphonic form. The score indeed carries the subtitle 'A Symphony' and it is quite possible to work out parallels between the six songs that make up the work and the normal four movements of the classical symphony. The second song ('The solitary one in Autumn') may for example be fitted into the place of the slow movement; the following song, 'Youth', into that of the scherzo. But the work as a whole is lyrical, not symphonic, and Mahler did not include it in the numbering of his symphonies. The texts of *Das Lied* are taken from German translations of Chinese poems, several of them by the famed Li-Tai-Po, and their choice and treatment reflects the general interest in oriental art and philosophy that existed in Europe at the beginning of the present century. Although the musical style is in the main the ripe Viennese romanticism of the later symphonies there are touches of exotic colour in instrumentation and texture, and the restrained sensuousness of such a song as 'Youth' is not out of keeping with the Chinese spirit.

Closely linked with *Das Lied* is the Ninth Symphony, for which it has been said that the title of the last song in *Das Lied*—'Farewell'—would have been entirely appropriate. It was written in the year following *Das Lied*, shares its atmosphere of nostalgia for lost youth and happiness, and is filled with the expression of human emotions in their primitive language of song and dance-rhythm. The second movement is cast in the form of a Ländler, the third is called *Rondo burleske*, and for a finale Mahler, like Tchaikovsky in his Sixth Symphony, writes a lament that disintegrates in the extremities of grief.

That Mahler did not feel that he had said his last word

in symphonic form is shown by his turning to it again in 1910, the year before his death, and planning a Tenth Symphony of which he left completed only a fragment, with sketches for two movements that were completed by Křenek and Berg for a performance at Vienna in 1924.

It is not unfitting that a book on nineteenth century composers should end with Mahler. He stands as the last great figure of the Viennese school that began with Mozart and Haydn and continued through Beethoven and Schubert. In his sensitiveness to human emotions, both within and without his own breast, in his longing for the return of a golden age of mankind and his search for a synthesis of artistic experience, he shows the final flowering of the romantic spirit. His music, like Elgar's, is always warm, opulent, spacious; the rhythmic and harmonic spareness and ruthlessness of Stravinsky and Bartók do not belong to his world. Yet the twentieth century makes its claims upon him. In the 'linear' style of his writing that prevailed from the Fifth Symphony onwards and reached its full development in the Ninth, he is the precursor of Schönberg; there are features of his tonality, especially in the Ninth Symphony, that show him veering away from the classical framework of major and minor, tonic and dominant, towards the twelve-tone system and even atonalism.

Of all composers of his period and stature he is the one who remains *sub judice*—the one major 'unplaced' composer of the nineteenth century. It may be, as some still insist, that his music shows an art in rapid process of decay, or at least decadence. But decadence in art is never final; it always contains the seeds of a new and unspoilt growth. We are already beginning to realise what Mahler has done, for good and ill, to the music that came after him. In time, too, will come fuller appreciation of what it is worth in and for itself.